AF540404

The Economic and Social Issues of MGNREGS: Dynamics of Rural Development in India

A Study of Nalgonda District in Telangana

The Economic and Social Issues of MGNREGS: Dynamics of Rural Development in India

A Study of Nalgonda District in Telangana

Dr. Donthagani Veerababu

A.P.H. PUBLISHING CORPORATION
4435–36/7, ANSARI ROAD, DARYA GANJ,
NEW DELHI-110002

Published by
S.B. Nangia
A.P.H. Publishing Corporation
4435–36/7, Ansari Road, Darya Ganj,
New Delhi-110002
Phone: 011–23274050
e-mail: aphbooks@gmail.com

2019

Typeset by
Ideal Publishing Solutions
C-90, J.D. Cambridge School,
West Vinod Nagar, Delhi-110092

Printed at
BALAJI OFFSET
Navin Shahdara, Delhi-110032

CONTENTS

ABOUT THE AUTHOR

Dr. Donthagani Veerababu is working as an Assistant Professor, at Department of Political Science, University of Hyderabad, Hyderabad, Telanagana state. He has been awarded Ph.D in Political Science and was Post-Doctoral fellow under the aegis of UGC-DSR-PDF from Osmania University, Hyderabad. He qualified Andhra Pradesh State Eligibility Test (AP SET) in Political Science. He was UGC-Meritorious Fellowship- New Delhi in 2009. He presented ten research papers in various national and international seminars; published more than fifteen articles on rural development in reputed national and international research journals. Dr. Veerababu writes editorials to leading Telugu newspapers on various social and political issues.

ABOUT THE BOOK

Human Development Strategy of MGNREGS is an attempt to understand the role of income for human and economic development in the over all growth of an individual.The key word is 'access' to income. Despite of the wealth in abundance, this country suffers from acute poverty. Since Independence, we notice that there has been an accumulation of wealth in a limited number of families and business households, the per capita distribution of income remains very low even now. India needs to prioritise the national well being of several individuals in the country. The Mahatma Gandhi National Rural Employment Guarantee Act (MGNREGA) is only a very nuanced initiative that was taken up by India

In India, The population explosion and the workforce in unorganised sector throws a major challenge to economic needs of the country. In fact, majority of the rural work force is also migrated to other cities in search of employment. In other terms, economic activities take place outside the cities with several fluctuations being involved due to the inclement weather. There was also a demand the programmes like NREGA are not leading to the asset creation.

After realizing the significance of public policy for public welfare and MGNREGS and its performance and its implications for the public welfare, a study entitled "The Economic and Social Issues of MGNREGS: A Policy Solution to Rural Poverty in India? A study of Nalgonda District in Telangana "assumes considerable amount of significance and relevance.

This book is based on the research work. It is useful to the students, scholars, policy makers and teachers in the area of rural development.

Chapter-1
INTRODUCTION

CONTEXT

John Stuart Mill characterised poverty alleviation as providing the most considerable amount of needful assistance, with the smallest encouragement to undue reliance on it. There is a long history of direct and targeted interventions to fight poverty in India through welfare schemes, subsidised food, farm-inputs, and credit subsidies. The Indian government wanted to ensure rural households to achieve a minimum income level which is cost-effective but without encouraging them to depend on public support. MGNREGS is the best example and Mahatma Gandhi had designed such a theory and a proposal for its practice.

To an extent, it could even be said that such a theory is close to, though not the same as, Keynes theory of stimulating an economy by generating effective demand. Further detailing is whose effective demand? Whose purchasing power? Gandhi's talisman was; "Whenever you are in doubt or when the self becomes too much with you, apply the following test; recall the face of the poorest and the weakest man whom you may have seen and ask yourself if the step you contemplate is going to be of any use to him".

In the current climate of globalisation, societies are experiencing rapid and profound changes in social and economic conditions. Consequently, decision-makers need a timely and objective analysis of economic and social conditions to understand these transformations. They have to provide a basis for broad and informed debate on public policy, and to establish a foundation for original policy formulation. The need is particularly acute because the social policy has not necessarily kept pace with the dramatic changes in economic policy. Government's at all levels have acknowledged the importance of redesigning public policy so that it meets the need of all the Indian poor and leads us towards more socially and economically sustainable communities. The extensive interrelatedness of inputs and outputs, the diversity of stakeholders, the quantum of resources committed and the extensiveness of results sought makes public policy decisions also very complicated. They are strategic as they involve a commitment of a large number of resources; have long gestation periods; outcomes are uncertain, and involve a certain degree of risk.

The adverse effects of globalisation are significant to justify an immediate policy response of additional labour market regulation and free social security programmes. The immediate effect of globalisation on the labour market is on salaried employment, wage earners and the poor. Due to the absence of adequate and timely availability of other types of employment in rural areas, agricultural labour remains a dominant form of employment opportunity. In rural areas, the pattern of employment has changed due to modern technology and non-farm employment. The key to employment planning in India lies in raising the productivity of the agricultural sector. Former Prime Minister of India Dr Manmohan Singh stated that there must be greater flexibility in labour markets without endorsing hire and fire; increasing growth and employment elasticity of growth is a concern. Employment has to generate from agro-processing, rural industries, and informal sectors. India has a labour cost advantage. However, there is a need for improving skills. Social security is a must, and the draft Employment Guarantee Act is a beginning in this direction. Sixty-seven per cent of the workforce is illiterate or semi-literate, and only 5 per cent workers in the 20 to 24 age-groups have skill jobs. No second opinion on the question of upgrading literacy, training and skills. However, it raises a policy question: who will perform these vocational training?

In India, the population explosion and the concomitant growth of the rural workforce are the issues in the employment scenario of our country. It is a significant challenge for India as it has to absorb the abundant people for better and productive means. Matters of great concern are the high incidence of poverty and unemployment in rural India. Rural areas are affected by low rate of agricultural growth and the rate of employment opportunities. Labour surplus countries like India need better labour-intensive technology with the potential to boost employment opportunities as well as the income of rural people. It is observed that the majority of the poor in rural areas of the county largely depends on the wages earned through manual, unskilled, and casual labour.

The agricultural labour market is a function of economic, social, and demographic variables rather than the meagre wage rate. In the choice of technology, labour intensive technology is better for labour surplus countries like India with the potential to boost employment opportunities as well as the income of the rural people. Severe issues in India are poverty, inequalities of income between the rural and urban and widening gap between the rich and the poor. In rural areas, economic activities are irregular and seasonal fluctuations resulting in periodic entry and withdrawal from the labour force. It is primarily on the part of marginal labourers and often women, who move back and forth between domestic work and productive work.

PORTFOLIO OF EMPLOYMENT PROGRAMS IN INDIA

To raise the per capita income and eradicate household poverty employment is a fundamental pre-requisite. Poor employment opportunity is one of the critical reasons for the endurance of rural and urban poverty in India. After independence and particularly from the Fifth Five Year Plan onwards, Government of India has initiated several rural development programmes for raising rural employment for the alleviation of rural poverty. A few critical among them are the Employment Guarantee Scheme (EGS); Rural Landless Employment Guarantee Programme (RLEGP); Food for

Work Programme (FWP); National Rural Employment Programme (NREP); Employment Assurance Scheme, Jawahar Rojgar Yojana (JRY), Sampoorna Gamin Rojgar Yojana (SGRY) and Swaijayanti Gram Swayrojgar Yojana (SGSY). Despite all these endeavours, unemployment in general and rural unemployment, in particular, has remained one of the critical issues of rural development. With an objective to alleviate the Government of India introduced rural poverty and employment generation programmes. Particular mentions are Employment cum Production Scheme, Food for Work Programme, Minimum Needs Programme and Twenty Point Programme. These programmes stress on providing health care, housing and education and nutrition facilities to the poor, particularly scheduled castes and tribes.

All these endeavours of raising employment through different schemes as well as the slowdown of the employment in agriculture have authenticated that rural unemployment is an abiding problem and cannot lie deciphered through piecemeal approaches. The seasonal nature of rural employment and low wage seasonal nature of rural employment and low wage rate has resulted in distressed migration of labour from the rural areas to urban areas and from the economically backward states to the economically developed states. It has hampered agriculture in the out-migrating states and added to the urban slums in the in-migrating states. Therefore, a strategic employment plan is a sine qua non for the eradication of rural poverty and prevention of distressed migration.

These all wage employment programmes were self-targeting with the objective to enhance livelihood security, especially to casual labourers. On account of some deficiencies, these programmes not succeeded to achieve primary objectives. Learning lessons from these programmes, the National Rural Employment Guarantee Act (NREGS) was enacted in parliament on 25th August 2005. The NREGS renamed as Mahatma Gandhi National Rural Employment Guarantee Act (MGNREGA) on 2nd October 2009. These programmes stress on health care, housing, education, and nutrition facilities poor, particularly to the scheduled castes and scheduled tribes.

MGNREGS and its Significance

The NREGS is implemented by the Ministry of Rural Development and is considered as the flagship programme of Central Government that affects the lives of the poor while promoting inclusive growth. National Rural Employment Guarantee Act (NREGA) was notified on September 7, 2005. It functioned under an act for rural employment in order to provide employment wherein other employment alternatives are scarce or inadequate. Coming into force on February 2, 2006, it was implemented in a phased manner. Phase-I (notified in 200 districts with effect from February 2nd 2006), Phase-II (extended to 130 districts in the financial year 2007-08, and 113 districts from April 1, 2007 and 17 districts of Uttar Pradesh with effect from May 15, 2007) and Phase III (remaining districts in all states and union territories from April 1, 2008).

The MGNREGS provides a legal guarantee of employment in rural places to one who is willing to perform casual manual labour as per the statutory minimum wage. Any adult applying for work under the Act is entitled to employment on public works within fifteen days. The National Advisory Council, guaranteed employment to an initial limit of hundred days per household annually, may be raised or removed whenever required. It would enable most poor households in rural India to cross the poverty line. MGNREGS is an opportunity to construct needful assets in rural areas. In particular, there is a massive potential for labour-intensive public works in the field of soil erosion, protection of forests, restoration of tanks, and related activities. Guaranteed employment is likely to change power equations in the rural society, and to foster a more equitable social order. In many states, people work at below the statutory minimum wage, which is rarely enforced the ground realities of rural employment. So, many non-poor agricultural workers could switch from existing agricultural employment to the MGNREGS.

The NREGS is a holistic measure aimed at fulfilling one of the most important Human Rights that is Right to Employment at least to one member of the family. One of the four goals of the National Rural employment Guarantee Act (NREGS) is the provision of a 'strong social safety net for the vulnerable groups by providing a fall-back employment source, when other employment alternatives are scarce or inadequate".

The main objective of NREGS is the creation of durable assets and strengthening the livelihood resource base of the rural poor for fighting poverty. Some of the salient features of the NREGS are as follows;(i) At least 100 days of employment for at least one able-bodied person in every rural household on asset creating public works programmes every year; (ii) Minimum wages on rate prevailing in states as per Minimum Wage Act-1948 and centre to step in if wages go up beyond minimum or less than rupees 60; (iii) Panchayats to finalize, approve implement and monitor the projects. The scheme shall not permit engaging any contractor for implementation of the projects; (iv) As far as practicable, a task funded under the scheme shall be performed by using manual labour and not machines; (v) A minimum of 33 per cent reservation to be made for women, where the number of applicant is very large; (vi) Every scheme shall certain adequate provisions for ensuring transparency and accountability at all level of implementation; (vii) All accounts and records relating to the scheme shall be made available for public scrutiny and any person desirous of obtaining a copy or relevant extracts there from may be provided such copies or extracts on demand and after paying such fee as may be specified in the scheme; and (viii) A copy of the muster rolls of each scheme or project under a scheme shall be made available in the offices of the Gram Panchayat and programme officer for inspection by any person interested after paying such fee as may be specified in the scheme.

The Employment Guarantee Scheme can also help to empower women, by giving them independent income-earning opportunities. MGNREGS provides that 30 percent of the employment provided, should be given to women. Implementation of MGNREGS has contributed to, very high levels of women empowerment, particularly in the following aspects that as the work is organized by women's groups, the gender perspective gets built in automatically. For the first time equal wages are really paid and this has boosted the earnings of women. As the bank deposits are increasing, the intra-household status of the woman has also been improving commensurately as she controls substantial cash resources and withdrawal can be only on her decision. Women's empowerment was not among the original intentions of the MGNREGS, and is not among its main objectives. However, provisions like priority for women in the ratio of one-third of total workers (Schedule 11(6)); equal wages for men and women (Schedule 11(34)); and crèches for the children of women workers (Schedule II (28)) were made in the Act: with the view of ensuring that rural women benefit from the scheme in a certain manner. Provisions like work within a radius of five kilometers from the house, absence of supervisor and contractor, and flexibility in terms of choosing period and months of employment were not made exclusively for women, but have, nevertheless, been conducive for rural women. Nevertheless, women have availed of the paid employment opportunity under MGNREGS in large numbers. Interestingly, this occurred largely spontaneously. The MGNREGS, the flag ship program of the UPA government was revolutionary in its promise of inclusive growth, the right to work and the dignity of labour and it was mostly delivered.

To a large extent the MGNREGS has got some impact on social structures. Wage payments through MGNREGS have initiated the biggest "financial inclusion" drive with requirement that all wage payments be made through banks and post offices.

It is also understood that for the first time, the power elite recognizes the peoples right to fight hunger with dignity, accepting that there labour will be the foundation for infrastructure and economic growth. It is also a fact that differently abled people are not being encouraged to do work appropriate to their abilities. It is observed that the single most important ingredient missing in the social audit attempts is the absence of strong political and administrative will.

Woman's participation under MGNREGS, measured in person-days, also exceeded their participation in erstwhile employment generation programmes like the Sampoorna Gamin Rojgar Yojana

(SGRY) and the Maharashtra Employment Guarantee Scheme (MEGS). There are wide variations across states; within states and across districts in the share of work days for women. At the national level the participation of women has increased significantly from 40.65 percent in 2006-07 to 47.72 percent in 2010-11

Table 1: Participation of Women under MGNREGS

Year	Total	Woman	Percentage
2006-07	9050.54	3679.01	40.65
2007-08	1437.95	6109.1	42.63
2008-09	21632.86	10357.32	47.87
2009-10	28359.57	13640.51	48.16
2010-11	25715.23	12274.21	47.72

Source: www nre.nic.com.in

Social Audit

Social audit is a governance instrument meant for raising transparency and accountability and minimizing corruption. With the decentralization and minimizing corruption. With the decentralization and devolution of functions functionaries and funds to the Panchayat raj institutions, the social audit has become inevitable. On the one hand, it will prevent skepticism of corruption against Panchayat and at the same time make the panchayats raj institutions accountable to the people.

Mahatma Gandhi NREGS earlier known as NREGS has strengthened the social auditing through various mechanisms adopted by the scheme which is mandated to be implemented by the village panchayats. One of the prime requirements of the scheme is that it is to be implemented by the village Panchayat not through the contractors either appointed by the panchayats or by the government. In this context, the social audit has become paramount importance.

SOCIAL AUDIT PROCESS IN MGNREGS IN ANDHRA PRADESH

The Government of Andhra Pradesh has spent excessively on various poverty alleviation programmes through various innovative programmes, despite this, only a fraction of population was able to get this amount. As a result, development schemes neglected the poor sections of the society who face these problems very frequently offered by such schemes. In majority of the cases, the rich sections of the rural populace corner the best that the government offers, whether it is in the form of wage employment, pensions, rural housing, land development, etc.

Andhra Pradesh is considered as one of the first few states in India to introduce social auditing system in development and -welfare programmes to curb the malpractices in the implementation of welfare initiatives. The social audit strategy in MGNREGS in Andhra Pradesh, had been designed to include the primary stakeholders (laborers working under the Employment Guarantee Scheme) in planning, decision-making, implementation, monitoring, evaluation and auditing-of the schemes. The social audit process begins with the filing of applications for information of relevant official records pertaining to the programme by trained civil society activists, who then identify literate youth from laborer's families. The youngsters are trained in the social audit processes and go into the rural areas and cross check official records through a door to door verification of works. Awareness building regarding the rights and entitlements of the laborers through focused group discussions is an integral part of the social audit process. And on a pre-notified date the reports along with the findings of the social audit are read out in public meetings attended by the laborers, official functionaries, political representatives and the media. The officials respond to the issues which are read out in public and take corrective action.

The Expected Outcome of Social Audit Process

The social auditing process, if conducted properly, expected to result in; (1) dissemination of information those Who need it; (ii) identify the malpractices in the delivery of schemes; (iii) pave the way for mid-course corrections; (iv) redresses the grievances of the laborers/participants; (v) unveil a culture of participation and openings in the implementation of the scheme; (vi) ensure horizontal accountability (it refers to the- host of mechanisms checks and balances internal to the state judicial oversight, auditing and accounting, performance incentives), through which state agencies are held to account; (vii) ensure vertical accountability (it refers to the mechanisms through which citizens hold the state to account); (viii) increased involvement of civil society in placing demands for accountability on the state etc. which are also the main features of the good governance.

Institutionalizing the Social Audit

The Department of Rural Development, Government of Andhra Pradesh has developed a team for managing social audit with the financial support of DFID (Department for International Development). The Rural Development Department has established Strategy and Performance Innovation Unit (SPIU), which provides the organisational backbone to the audit process. The SPIU is headed by a Director, who is drawn from state civil service cadre. The Director is assisted by a team of 25 resource persons as well as social development specialists, who are exclusively drawn from civil society, in the social audit process to ensure a high degree of autonomy and objectivity to the exercise and also serve as checks and balances in the implementation of the schemes.

The Director SPIU and the social development specialists are responsible for taking several policy and management decisions related to the conduct of social audits on MGNREGS. The Stare Resource Persons (SRPs) are responsible for managing the day today aspects of conducting social audit. This includes drawing up the social audit schedule, training district level resource persons, coordinating with district level officials and ensuring follow up social audit findings. The District Resource Persons (DRPs) are responsible for managing the action conduct of the social audit, This includes identifying the Village Social Auditors (VSAS) (2-4 persons per village), training the VSAs, filling RTI applications for assessing government departments and interacting with the mandal level officials to organize logistics and public hearings.

Social Audit Unit: The Government of Andhra Pradesh had initiated a separate unit exclusively for social audit called Andhra Pradesh Society for Social Accountability and Transparency (APSSAT) with adequate autonomy from the government. The unit consists of experts and activists from civil society organizations chosen to spearhead the initiative across the state. The unit supports the social audit initiatives through technical and knowledge inputs, training and capacity to control and manage hundreds of social audits undertaken in the state.

Gram Sabha as a Social Audit Forum

Article 17 (1) of the MGNREGS says Gram Sabha would monitor all works/ schemes which are implemented in the gram Panchayat. Further, Article 17(2) of the MGNREGS stipulates that the Gram Sabha shall conduct regular social audits of all the projects under the scheme taken up within the Gram Panchayat. Article 17(3) says the Gram Panchayat shall make available all relevant documents including the muster rolls, bills, vouchers, measurement, books, copies of sanction orders and other connected books of accounts and papers to the Gram Sabha for the purpose of conducting the social audit. The guidelines of Ministry of Rural Development, Government of India, indicates that there should be continuous monitoring and as well as six monthly social audit through gram sabha called social audit forum.

As per the MGNREGS guidelines, the process of social audit should include public vigilance and verification of the following 11 stages of' implementation of the schemes. They are: registration of families; distribution of cards; receipts of work applications; preparation of shelf of projects and selection of sites; development and approval of technical estimates and issuance of works; payment of unemployment allowance; payment of wages; evaluation of work; mandatory social audit in Gram Sabha. All these stages would promote transparency and accountability of the administration in the implementation of the schemes.

Maintenance of Records/Registers

The maintenance of reports and records by the Panchayat is one of the important prerequisites of the social audit. It will provide both the functionaries as well as the people of the village panchayats to see the report and records when they want, so that any doubts regarding the receipt of fund and utilization of fund under the NREGS scheme by the Panchayat is cleared then and there. As it is a tied fund strictly used for the purpose for which it is earmarked, therefore the maintenance of records and registers become further imperative. It is usually observed that panchayats many times complain non-payment of their residuary bills due to the over/under utilisation of funds in the coresonding period.

With wages for employment under the MGNREGS being compulsorily paid through bank accounts, this has brought more people under the ambit of the banking system than any other government scheme. The Mahatma Gandhi National Rural Employment Guarantee Act, which is considered as the biggest-ever inclusion initiative undertaken in the country. With wages for employment under the MGNREGS being compulsorily paid through bank accounts, the impact of this has been that the quantum of money which has actually raised the hands of the poor has been much higher than what it used to be and this has impacted the rural economy in a very positive manner. During the recent global financial crisis, growth in the country's rural areas continued to be logged at about 14 per cent because the consumption power of the people in the rural areas did not significantly go down. The NREGS increased the livelihood security of households in the rural areas by providing a minimum of 100 days of guaranteed wage employment in every financial year to every household whose adult members volunteer to do unskilled manual work. The eradication of corruption has become a major concern in the implementation of National Rural Employment Guarantee Scheme (NREGS).

One of the most salient and characteristic feature of NREGA is breaking away from the age old practice of engaging contractors with a complete ban on the practice. The local contractors, who were responsible for providing all material, labour, equipment and other services necessary often ended up exploiting the labourers. These labourers are often from Rural poor household constituting both men and women alike get trapped in a vicious cycle of exploitation. These labourers are often deprived with even basic human rights and with no or little audit get paid far too less for their services rendered.

Enter NREGA, the flagship program of the government bans the use of such entitlements enjoyed by the contractors with a complete ban on them and putting in place an excellent framework where in labourers get a guarantee of minimum wages and provides legal entitlements to labourers ranging from minimum working hours to various creche facilities like adequate rest, good drinking water facilities, proper safety measures at work places as well as proper medical aid. One of the biggest attraction being the unemployment allowance being paid to the labourers in spite there is no work of the guaranteed days of work. Thus, NREGA is a visionary program which is incomparable with other government programmes where corrupt officials and contractors work in tandem with contractor eyeing maximization of profits and bribe officials. NREGA is a program where local people are at all stages – planning, implementation and social audit.

The very idea of involving local people in effective planning, implementation and audit gives a new ray of hope for effective rural governance in India. One of the key problem destroying the fabric of Indian democracy is the failing of systems of system delivery and program implementation. The failure of the public sector in rural development is turning into a threat for very existence of poor in independent India. This failure has indeed failing rural life over the last 60 years and is getting worse with each passing time. If provisions of NREGA is implemented effectively it can bridge the gap which was lacking all these years.

Every government since India got independence main concern is corruption and corruption in NREGA being a government scheme, is no exception. Through adequate measures and checks in place like public disbursal of wages, distribution of job cards and its maintenance and effective social audits, corruption is in check yet NREGA remained vulnerable to fraud and cash embezzlement. The main concern being the lack of division between implementing agency and payment agency under payment of cash, wherein the implementing agency which consisted of middlemen, private enterprises created bogus job cards, inflated muster rolls and pocketed the wages being paid to labourers. The introduction of direct benefit transfer, wherein payments to labourers under NREGA is directly credited to their bank and post office accounts separated the payment agency from implementing agency thus curbing corruption significantly. But yet there is corruption through manipulating workers salary through deception, colliding with staffs of bank and post office and indulging in corruption and even through extortion by forcing workers to part with extra wages sent illegally.

NREGA being a breakthrough scheme introduced by the government also ensures the Milennium Development Goals in the field of environmental sustainability and NREGA's salient feature is that it strikes a balance between human action and natural resources can be seen as an ecological act. While NREGA act aims at eradication of extreme poverty at the same time it plays the role of ecological act by making villages self-sufficient through productive assets creation such as water tanks, soil conservation works, recharging ground water increasing percolation of rain water, reducing soil erosion, increase in soil fertility, conservation of biodiversity resulting in regenerating natural resource base which in turn will result in sustainable livelihood for residents. Thus NREGA not only is seen as an effective tool to fight poverty but also contribute to ecological restoration through its design. The main goal of NREGA activities is to conserve natural resources and maintain ecological services to sustain food and livestock balance, increase grass and forest production. The benefits reaped from activities implemented under NREGA can be turned as "Services Provided". The millennium ecosystem assessment (MEA-2005) considers humans as an integral component of the natural ecosystem unlike classical approaches, which differentiates humans as non-natural out of nine works which are preferred under MGNREGS, 7 focuses on soil and water conservation.

The order of priority for the areas of works are

- -Conservation and harvesting of water
- -Afforestation and plantation of trees to full-proof drought situation

- -Major and Minor irrigation canals
- -Provisions of irrigation facility to the beneficiaries under the Indira AwasYojana of Govt of India and land owned by SC and ST's households
- -Rejuvenation of water bodies
- -Development of land
- -Controlling of flood and protection works
- -Rural connectivity through all-weather access
- -Any other works, which may be notified by the central government in consultation with the state government.

With such work the ecological foundations of sustainable agriculture are strengthened. The MGNREGS is probably the world's largest ecological security program. The main factor of this scheme is the involvement of local people in every decision ranging from what kind of works need to be done and selection of work sites to project implementation and auditing of works. It therefore strengthens the roots of the democratic process by effective decentralization at the basic level by incorporating gram sabhas in their planning and decision making.

The Role of MGNREGA in Creating Sustainable Assets

With good planning and well execution, studies have shown that investment for MGNERGS assets have maximum return in turn of benefits. While, studies have also shown certain technical problems ans issues with design quality which question the potential of these works MGNERGA has faced both praise as well as criticism. Critics argue that works undertaken are Non-durable and are not good -and only positive outcome from this act is employment generation. On the other -hand, scholars argue that if well planned, designed and constructed even earthen works are durable. Three parameters have been used to study the quality, durability and utility of the MGNERGA assets – Cost recovery, beneficiary perception-based surveys and sound technical design. However, these three categories are inter-related for example beneficiary perceptions and technical design have often been used to estimate cost. Further other than these three categories and out of it perception-based surveys also use assessment, payment of wages and timely measurement of planning.

Total works taken up under MGNREGP FY 2006-07 to FY 2011-12*

S. No	Type of works	Total number of works completed from FY 2006-07 to FY 2011-12* (In Lakhs)	On going works (In Lakhs)	% of total works taken up from FY 2006-07 to FY 2011-12*
1	Water conservation and water harvesting (e. g: farm ponds, percolation tanks etc.)	19.5	36.4	25
2	Flood control and protection (e. g. check dams, culverts, etc.)	3.9	5.9	4
3	Drought proofing (e.g. afforestation/ tree plantation, agro-forestry, etc.)	5.2	13.0	9
4	Irrigation canals (macro and micro irrigation works, etc.)	5.7	9.5	7
5	Renovation of traditional bodies (desalting of tanks etc.)	6.6	9.8	7
	Total water conservation and water-related works (sum of (i) to (v) above)	**40.9**	**74.7**	**51**

S. No	Type of works	Total number of works completed from FY 2006-07 to FY 2011-12* (In Lakhs)	On going works (In Lakhs)	% of total works taken up from FY 2006-07 to FY 2011-12*
6	Works on lands of SC/ST/BPL/ SMF and IAY and land reform beneficiaries	13.0	19.9	14
7	Land development (e. g. contour bunds, field bunds, etc.)	13.9	18.8	13
8	Rural connectivity (e. g. village roads, etc.)	16.0	28.3	19
9	Others (e. g. Bharat Nirman Kendras)	2.08	4.6	3
	Total works	**86.6**	**146.3**	**100**

* Provisional data: at the time of the preparation of the report data entry for states was still open for the year 2011-12.

Source: Mahatma Gandhi National Rural Employment Guarantee Act (official Web site), http://www.mgnrega.nic.in.

Preventing Migration: MGNERGA to a great extent creates ample employment opportunity and secures livelihood of a significant rural population thereby stopping seasonal migration as well as permanent migration which was the case until this scheme came into existence.

Controlling spread of HIV/AIDS: NREGS also has the potential to address other major sociological issues like the spread of AIDS, stop farmers suicides etc. since migration of rural population is one of the leading causes for the spread of AIDS.

Transforming rural economic and social relations: It is quite evident that the scheme has huge potential to transform rural economic and social relations at many levels. With at least 33% participation of women as mandated by the act results in social economic empowerment of women. With significant participation of women as well as significant increase in women's paid work, there are substantial social changes as well. With enough participation of woman, family distress migration comes down and improvement of nutrition levels in children and family underprivileged come under Financial Inclusion since bank and post office accounts are mandatory for payment of NREGA. Thus, NREGA has a great potential as a complete inclusive program in many ways.

Administrative Arrangements for Implementation

MGNREGA scheme is being implemented at different levels right from national, state, district up to the Mandal and village level and various institution and agencies are also involved.

The Ministry of Rural Development is the nodal agency for formulating acts and scheme implementation at the national level. All the rules, regulations, procedures are planned and also the ministry provides adequate resources, support, timely review, monitoring and evaluation of the scheme at the state government level. The ministry has established Management Information System (MIS) for complete and comprehensive information and coverage of the program in the country.

A separate council has been established – The central employment guarantee council (CEGC) which advises the ministry on wage related queries and also responsible for effective planning and implementation and creating annual reports on the implementation of the scheme and submit the same to parliament.

At the state level, the state government formulates the scheme and rules and regulation are implemented in consonance with the central government. A separate officer at the rank of commissioner is appointed to oversee the scheme and carry out objectives laid down in the act. The ministry of rural development of the state government is made nodal agency for the implementation of the scheme. The ministry also prepares budget and oversees whether the budget is released on time and provides administrative, finance and technical support to the district level agencies involved in scheme implementation. The act also provides for establishment of a state employment guarantee council at the state level to work in tandem with the centre.

The Act also provides -for the establishment of a State Employment Guarantee Council at the state level to advise the state governments on the implementation of the scheme and to undertake monitoring and evaluation of the activities, prepare the annual reports and submit the same to the state legislature.

At the district level Zilla Parishad (ZP) is the principal agency for planning, implementation, monitoring and supervision of the scheme. The District Collector acts as the District Programme Coordinator (DPC) of the scheme and is responsible for preparation of budget. The Project Director, District Water Management Agency (DWMA) act as Additional District Programme Coordinator and assists the DPC in overall management of the programme through an EGS unit. In addition, the Chief Executive Officer (CEO) Zilla Parishad, Project Director, District Rural Development Agency (DRDA) and Project Officer Integrated Tribal Development Agency (ITDA) (in agency areas) are also designated as the Additional District Project Coordinators (ADPC) of the programme.

At the mandal level, Mandal Patishad Development Officer (MPDO) assisted by three technical assistants is made responsible for monitoring and implementation of the scheme. As the Chief Coordinator of the programme, the MPDO is expected to extend necessary support,- administrative and otherwise, to Gram Panchayats under his/her control, scrutinizes the EGS plans of Gram Panchayat and ensures that such plans meet the employment demand of the village. He/she also oversees that all the agencies involved in the scheme start their work on time and workers receive their entitlements.

At the village level Gram Panchayat is the primary unit for planning and implementation of the scheme. It is thought that Gram Panchayats would function on the recommendations of the respective Ward Committees and Gram Sabha of the village. The individual member/groups who want to avail of the benefits/wage employment under the scheme are required to register their name with the Gram

Panchayat. Identification of eligible adult member, issuance of job cards and its actual implementation are the three phases identified in the process of implementation of the scheme. The Panchayat Secretary supported by the field assistant is made responsible for registration, issuance of job cards and implementation of the scheme.

The NREGS envisages that all the developmental departments are expected to involve in the district in the implementation of the scheme. The district administration prepares the plan and executes the scheme in such a way that supervision and monitoring of the scheme would be carried out at the constituency, mandal and at the village levels simultaneously and all the concerned officials are involved in the implementation of the scheme. The senior officers of the district are appointed as Special Officers (SOs) to supervise and coordinate the work at constituency level. For each mandal, Monitoring Officers are appointed for overall supervision and execution of the works.

GOVERNANCE AND PROCESS CHALLENGES

Awareness and planning

There is low awareness among potential beneficiaries about certain provisions of the MGNREGA. This limits their ability to fully benefit under the Act. Infrequent meetings and low participation at the Gram Sabhas (GS) convened for planning MGNREGA works further limit the implementation of the scheme at the village level in many places.

Awareness about the Act

- Low awareness about unemployment allowance
- Low awareness about work on demand
- Low awareness about grievance redressal mechanisms
- Issue of dated receipts and non provision of work within 15 days
- Unemployment allowance
- Delay in payments
- Inadequate staff

- Irregular flow of funds
- Poor coverage/network of banks/post offices
- Non-streamlined record-keeping at banks/post offices
- Illiterate workers
- Low cash and line limit

RECENT INITIATIVES TO STRENGTHEN MGNREGS

List of permissible works expanded

The list of permissible works under MGNREGA has been expanded:

- To strengthen the positive synergy between MGNREGP and agriculture and allied rural livelihoods.
- To respond to the demands of the states for greater location-specific flexibility in permissible works, and to help improve the ecological balance in rural India.

Some of these works are new but many of them come within the category of works already permitted under MGNREGA. The list was drawn up in response to demands from states for a more elaborate, specific and unambiguous list of works that could be taken up under the categories currently permissible.

While taking up works under MGNREGP, the following conditions need to be followed:

- Only those works to taken up that result in creation of durable assets,
- The order of priority of works will be determined by the Gram Panchayat (GP),
- 60:40 ratio for labour: material cost should be maintained at the GP level,
- No0 contractors/ labour-displacing machinery to be used.
- Ensuring the demand based character of MGNREGP
- Effective planning
- Strict time schedule

- Deployment of human resources
- Reducing delays in wage payments
- Strengthening Management Information System
- Equal opportunity for vulnerable groups
- Facilitation
- Greater role for civil society organizations
- Better social audits and vigilance for transparency and accountability
- Vigilance cell
- Strengthening section 25 of the Act
- Limitations on Administrative expenses

STATEMENT OF THE RESEARCH PROBLEM

Human Development Strategy of MGNREGS is an attempt to understand the role of income for human and economic development in the over all growth of an individual.The key word is 'access' to income. Despite of the wealth in abundance, this country suffers from acute poverty. Since Independence, we notice that there has been an accumulation of wealth in a limited number of families and business households, the per capita distribution of income remains very low even now. India needs to prioritise the national well being of several individuals in the country. The Mahatma Gandhi National Rural Employment Guarantee Act (MGNREGA) is only a very nuanced initiative that was taken up by India. For example, Japan through its various economic policies had lifted several millions out of the poverty. The policies pursued by Japanese had drastically reduced the rural-urban divide. Accumulated income was accessible to all its citizens by various policies. Further, the distribution of the accumulated wealth was not done properly by other major powers include Brazil, India, China etc. If enhancing the well-being of people is the priority, then ask the question 'how is it possible to access to income'. Mere distribution of income for a short-term period is not the answer. The policies pursued with.

Though growth rates have gone high in recent years but the growth is perceived to have excluded disadvantaged groups of Scheduled Castes (SCs), Scheduled Tribes (STs), minorities and women as Indian society is stratified in terms of social, economic-and human capital endowments. It is now believed that rapid economic growth could exacerbate pre-existing inequalities rather than narrowing them in an inclusive way and hence, inclusive growth (wherein people contribute to and benefit from economic growth) policies are needed. Given the persistent inequalities in the access to public infrastructure and social services such as education and health, it is believed that decentralized institutions can play a significant role in fostering inclusive growth. The Eleventh Five-Year Plan sought to substantially empower and use Panchayat Raj Institutions (PRIs) that include Zilla Panchayat, Taluk Panchayat and Gram Panchayat, as the primary means of delivering essential services that are critical to inclusive growth.

The population explosion and the workforce in unorganised sector throws a major challenge to economic needs of the country. In fact, majority of the rural work force is also migrated to other cities in search of employment. In other terms, economic activities take place outside the cities with several fluctuations being involved due to the inclement weather. There was also a demand the programmes like NREGA are not leading to the asset creation.

After realizing the significance of public policy for public welfare and MGNREGS and its performance and its implications for the public welfare, a study entitled **"Rural Development and National Rural Employment Guarantee Scheme: A study of Nalgonda District in Andhra Pradesh"**assumes considerable amount of significance and relevance.

OBJECTIVES OF THE STUDY

1. To examine the socio- economic profile of the beneficiaries of the MGNREGS program.
2. To explain the perceptions of elite respondents about the performance of MGNRGS in the study area.

3. To analyze the beneficiary perceptions about the functioning of MGNREGS.
4. To understand the challenges (Man power and resources, rigorous tracking and monitoring for effectiveness, coordination mechanism for convergence and the responsive in the delivery system) confronting the implementation processes of MGNREGS.
5. To discuss the expectations of the beneficiaries of MGNREGS.

HYPOTHESES OF THE STUDY

1. The performance of MGNREGS is socially neutral.
2. Governance practices in MGNREGS are poor.

Towards the end of the objectives and hypotheses mentioned, the following methodology is adopted.

SAMPLE DESIGN

For the purpose of the present study, 200 households covered under MGNREGS are selected mostly by adhering to the principles of stratified random sampling. The criteria of stratification are place, and social status. The place and social status profile of the sample beneficiaries are presented below.

Table-1

place	Frequency	Percent	Cumulative Percent
palavaram	40	20.0	20.0
Pedda Ravulapally	40	20.0	40.0
Goodapoor	40	20.0	60.0
Mallaprajpally	40	20.0	80.0
Chirumarthy	40	20.0	100.0
Total	200	100.0	

SOURCES OF DATA

The present study makes use of both primary and secondary sources of data. The sources of secondary data included records of

Panchayat offices of concerned villages and reports of the district planning officer concerned. The primary data are collected directly from the respondents by administering a pre designed questionnaire/ schedules.

PERIOD OF THE STUDY

The present study made use of the data of MGNREGS programs in the sample villages for the year 2012-13 and the necessary data were collected from October-December of 2012.

SCOPE OF THE STUDY

The present study confines itself to evaluate the performance of MGNREGS in Nalgonda district of Andhra Pradesh and does not cover the said program in other parts of Andhra Pradesh.

TECHINQUES OF ANALYSIS

The present study made use of interview method to collect the data. Simple percentages, frequencies, and other relevant techniques are used.

Chapter-2

REVIEW OF THE LITERATURE

A modest attempt is made to review the earlier studies in order to identify the aspects covered and identify the gaps if any.

Onokerhoraye, A.G (1981)[1] has opined that the techniques of rural development are still not fully developed in Nigeria. More knowledge is required of than interactions between policies, institutions and technology. The objectives of the rural development are not static, they change over time, and many projects designed for one period may not meet the needs of the future. Many projects have also suffered from inadequate knowledge of the appropriate forms of administrative institutions and of the socio-cultural and institutional environment in which they are operated. Much can be done therefore, through social research progress report in rural development in Nigeria can be achieved only by continual and searching criticism of approaches and methods. The quality and relevance of the volume of the research and public policy on rural development in Nigeria have suffered seriously from lack of such criticism.

Mulligan, Casey B. et. Al (2004)[2] has stated that their studies in sociology, economics and political science have found little impact of democracy on particular public policies. It is found

---

1 Onokerhoraye, A.G, "Perspective of public policy and social research in rural development in Nigeria", QUARTERLY JOURNAL OF ADMINISTRATION, 15(3), 1981(April): 183-192

2 Mulligan, Casey B. et. Al, "Do democracies have different public policies than nondemocracies?", JOURNAL OF ECONOMIC PERSPECTIVES, 18(1), 2004(Winter): 51-74

that there is an obvious raw correlation between democracy and the introduction of pension and welfare programs (raw correlations like these are obvious in our data, too), but pointed out the economic development likely drives social Programs and is correlated with democracy. Holding constant proxies for a country's age and income, they found democracies and non democracies to be pretty similar in terms of their likelihood of introducing a Social Program. In a study of European and advanced South American countries about a century ago holding constant country age and income, the average democracy was similar to the average non democracy in terms of spending on public pensions, welfare, unemployment and health. It is further evident that little democracy-non democracy difference in terms of the details of how public pension Programs obtain revenue and how they disburse it. Despite improvements in the measurement of democracy, control variables and pubic policies, accumulation of more years of data and examination of case studies we still find no significant partial correlation between democracy and the amount of spending on pensions or welfare. We add several economic and social policy out come measures, with an emphasis on instruments of rich-poor redistribution, including education spending, the corporate income tax rate, personal income tax flatness and whether the payroll tax is capped, and find only one of them to differ between economically and demographically similar democracies and non democracies. The one difference is that democracies tend to have flatter (and thereby less redistributive) personal income taxes. We offer an economic interpretation of these findings. As compared with the economic and social policies in authoritarian countries, democratic policies do not seem to ignore the intensity of policy preferences nor to reflect a significantly more equal distribution of political Power. Economic and social policies in all kinds of countries are to a first approximation the outcome of tradeoffs-like efficiency, or conflicts among generations, or among industries and occupations that are basic to human nature and not specific to particular political institutions.

Harrison, Elizabeth (2012)[3] has observed that in public participation in healthcare in the United Kingdom, governmentality achieves its effects by resting on the apparently freely chosen preferences of self-regulating "active citizens". However, such choices are in fact considerably more curtailed than is suggested in participatory discourse. Shaw (2011) discusses this in relation to community development more generally in the United Kingdom, arguing that increasingly, a "performance culture" has been rolled out through various standardized versions of community engagement, which are steered and controlled by those in power. She suggests that in the process, the voices of the least powerful are too often reduced to a "dutiful whisper" or what Hodgson (2004) has called the "manufacture of consensus". In the second part of this paper, he suggests that it is necessary to nuance approaches to governmentality, which stress power binaries and underplay the role of resistance and identity. There are limits to the analytical power of the idea governmentality in much the same way as there are limits to the ability of one set of actors to govern another. This is because the treatment of power in the concept of governmentality still tends towards binary division, however much resistance is theoretically entailed. One of these divisions is the entrenched and immovable interests implied by the "invited/inviters" distinction. It is easy to overstate the partnership relationship in a way that understates the agency of the "invited" or presents this as simple and unchanging. The power of the concept of governmentality that it draws attention to hierarchies and exclusions created by participatory projects and the limited possibilities for resistance. However, the consequences of participatory processes are not predetermined, nor are its subjects completely controlled, nor always easy to manage. In the case I have described, not only is there subversion and resistance, but the divide between inviters and invited turned out to be considerably more complex than might be assumed. In this, people occupy complex and sometimes shifting identity positions. Their identity is in turn partially shaped by the apparent power that they encounter and their responses to this. It is, therefore, very important

3 Harrison, Elizabeth, "Performing partnership: Invited participation and older people's forums, "HUMAN ORGANIZATION, 71(2), 2012(Summer): 157-166

to interrogate the circumstances in which partnerships take place and particularly to the ways in which choices are made and shaped in such partnership. Whether partnership and participation are "given" or "claimed" is one critically important aspect of this.

Vasanthi, Nimushakavi (2011)[4] has opined that the issue of regulation of domestic work must necessarily be addressed through public policy choices that the state makes. So far we have chosen to allow domestic work to remain unrecognized and a private matter. This neglect spills over to paid domestic work. The survey results indicate that legal strategies in terms of fixing minimum wages have not had much impact. This leads to two conclusions; one that wage fixation alone does not result in the worker receiving the wage; the other, that wage fixation does not have a detrimental effect on employment. The survey showed that workers did receive more than the minimum wage even without being aware of it. This depended on the location of the workplace and the bargaining power of the worker. After two years of wage notification, no impact on employment was indicated. The argument that wage fixation would lead to a fall in demand made by the state is not borne out. The lack of classification of work is another reason for little impact on wages. The specific situations of domestic workers in terms of recognition of the home as the workplace, the classification of workers, the need for a recognition of a wide set of rights including privacy and forced labour at the workplace, the identification of the hazards of work, the need to provide for appropriate social security schemes and other mechanisms still remain to be addressed.

The use of a rights framework to understand discrimination and state action such as the Convention on the Elimination of All Forms of Discrimination against Women (CEDAW) might help in highlighting the gravity of the situation. The CEDAW provides for a broad spectrum of rights for women against discrimination. State parties to the convention are required to identify the barriers

4 Vasanthi, Nimushakavi, "Addressing paid domestic work: A public policy concern.
ECONOMIC AND POLITICAL WEEKLY, 46(43), 2011(October): 85-93

faced by women to equal participation and enjoyment of rights and address them. Discrimination perpetuated by state inaction could be said to be a systematic violation of rights of women. It has been argued that in the case of domestic workers employed by diplomats in Germany, that the failure of the state to protect and promote the rights of these workers could be understood as a systematic violation by a state party inviting an inquiry procedure into that country's practices. A similar argument could be made in the case of all domestic workers who face neglect, exclusion and exploitation as a result of state inaction to protect and promote their rights. The human rights framework helps in understanding the exploitation of domestic workers in wider terms than the need for employment law protection. The association with servitude, racial connotations and caste-based occupations highlights the serious violations of fundamental human rights far wider than the denial of minimum wages and hours of work.

The other framework useful in understanding public policy interventions is the recognition and redistributive justice framework enunciated by Nancy Fraser. The idea as used in the context of class, caste and gender intersections in domestic work is to value domestic work quite independently of conditions of work and wages through suitable legislative interventions or the redistributive.

The absence of such an approach of recognition going hand in hand with redistribution is demonstrated by the lack of assessment of the skills and efforts that go into domestic work. The manner in which various legislations have excluded domestic workers reveals the biases in public policy that effect domestic workers.

The workers interviewed expected a wider intervention from law which included range of benefits like ration cards, education and housing. The most important expectation from the law was on improving wages. Legislation on domestic workers needs to be integrated with broader interventions such as recognition of a set of social rights in education, housing and health. Legislative interventions, which result in the rigidity of the labour market by introducing restrictions on entry into the work, might produce negative results. This might result in denying employment to those who need it most. It is well-documented that the informal sector workers ape economically fragile and any legislative interventions must take into account that their sustenance is not harmed in anyway. A broader agenda to provide recognition to domestic workers as workers and to change cultural stereotypes regarding work to enhance the visibility of domestic work as a form of work is called for. This recognition has been denied to domestic workers by not including them as workers in most labour legislations on social protection. In order to extend the powers of the labour department to conduct inspections at the workplaces of domestic workers, the home must be seen as a workplace, which will need a changed perception towards domestic work. Similarly, access to courts, dispute resolution mechanisms, protections against termination of employment by specifying the grounds of dismissal, inclusion within the ambit of workers for maternity protection and legislations extending protection for women, such as the pending protection of women from sexual harassment bill, are all steps towards a greater visibility to domestic workers.

Ananth, S (2012)[5] has explained the regulatory maze that awaits the microfinance industry in terms of public policy challenge. How ever, it is imperative to note that a business can hope to succeed only when they have a sustainable business model that does not collapse under its own weight at the smallest shock. Unfortunately, the industry seems to have failed to realize the inherent instability in their business model and instead prefer to blame public policy for their present troubles.

Kundu, Amit (2013)[6] has observed that the recommendation of NCEUS government should take proper initiative to reduce gender discrimination in the agricultural labour market of India

5 Ananth, S, "Regulating microfinance: A challenge for public policy", INDIAN JOURNAL OF PUBLIC ADMINISTRATION, 58(2), 2012, (April-June): 184-196

6 Kundu, Amit, "Effective public policy which can reduce gender discrimination in the agricultural labour market: A theoretical investigation", ASIAN ECONOMIC REVIEW, 55(3), 2013(December): 429-442

both in terms of wage and employment. The following steps can be taken by the government to combat that labor market discriminating problem.

(1) Representation of female agricultural laborer should be included in the committee of Dispute Resolution council at district level and conciliation committee at block or Panchayat level. This can improve the probability that the employer is apprehended and punished for violating the social security norm.

(2) The size of penalty should be high. As the size is decided in the meeting of the Conciliation Committee, the employer will be fully, aware of that and there is no question of informational gap. So the non-complying farmer cum employer even if enjoying monopsony power in the labour market wants to minimize the gap between in order to avoid the expected cost on penalty.

(3) Actually it is difficult to reduce employment discrimination between the male and female agricultural laborers because the employer farmer has a belief that a male agricultural laborer is comparatively more productive than a female agricultural laborer. Still it is here proved that under certain conditions high 'k' is comparatively more effective to reduce not only wage discrimination but also employment discrimination marginally.

Datt, G. and Ravallion, M (1994)[7] has proposed an empirical approach to estimating the impact on intra-household time allocation of employment on public-works projects. The model explains time allocation conditional on public-works employment, which is allowed to be endogenous, when suitable tests reject erogeneity. The statistical implementation is for two villages in the state of Maharashtra in India. Behavioral responses differ markedly between the villages. In Shirapur

7 Datt, G. and Ravallion, M, "Transfer benefits from public-works employment:Evidence for rural India", ECONOMIC JOURNAL, 104(427), 1994 (November): 1346-1369

wealthier households participate less in the projects, though there are signs that social stigmas and work disabilities dilute targeting performance somewhat. There is little sign of such effects in Kanzara. In both villages, employment in the projects is generally exogenous to time allocation, suggesting that the ideal embodied in the EGS of providing such work on demand is not being met. This confirms time-series evidence in Ravallion et al. (1993).The one exception to the erogeneity finding is for unemployment. This is consistent with the rationing of available public employment according to (in part) unemployment in other activities. In Shirapur, where a gender desegregation of the model is feasible, there are signs of significant gender cross-effects in time allocation, such as through men taking up more own-farm work when women join the project sites. The projects also displace different activities for different genders unemployment for men, leisure/domestic work for women. Our results suggest that the pecuniary opportunity cost to public-works participants is low, through this is more true of Shirapur, where participation is also higher. Overall, the projects do appear to generate sizeable net income gains to participants, certainly far greater than implied by using market wage rates for similar work to value the forgone income.

Urzua, Raul (2000)[8] has opined that weather we like or not, international migration will continue. While the free movement of the people is still right for which we are not prepared, and perhaps never will understand the peaceful existence of the people from different regions and cultures are essential in today's new and still emerging global society. This also constitutes a major challenge for the social sciences. Like the problems creation this challenge, it cannot be taken up by a single country or a single discipline; international interdisciplinary cooperation is crucial. Improving sources of data, sponsoring comparative research projects and

8 Urzua, Raul, " Internatinal migration, social science, and public policy ", INTERNATIONAL SOCIAL SCIENCE JOURNAL, 165, 2000, (September): 421-430

changing curricula and training programmes, while establishing the necessary networks for the purpose, are tasks that we just cannot put off.

Seroka, Jim (1987)[9] has found that there is considerable variation among rural counties with respect to their governmental leader's positions in support of innovation and modernization of administrative procedures and programmes. Rural American leaders neither completely support nor oppose change in administrative procedures and programmes. Second, a significant factor in the variation is the combined demographic and economic environment of the rural community. As reflected by this pattern of responses to the survey, the need for programme expansion and the availability of resources to expand programmes and services are important in attempting innovation. Moreover, when either need or resources is tacking, the propensity to support administrative innovation falls dramatically. Finally, when both need and resources are lacking, rural leader support for administrative innovation becomes even weaker.

The findings reported in this note may have serious implications for the development of rural administrative capacity building in the United States. Barring concerted federal or cooperative state action, inequalities in administrative capacity among rural communities are likely to increase. The rural communities which have grown the most in recent years are in the best position and are most willing to improve their administrative capacity, and thus will be able to capitalize and extend that growth into the future. Those communities least affected by growth have leaders which are least disposed to develop the infrastructure to reverse that trend. In other words, without external governmental intervention, growing rural communities will continue to grow, while declining communities may decline even further.

---

9 Seroka, Jim, "Rural community growth patterns and policy-maker attitudes towards administrative innovation",COMMUNITY DEVELOPMENT JOURNAL, 22(2), 1987(April):131-134

Ownen, Robert et.al (2002)[10] have looked at four different perspectives on the diffusion of innovation which might present different perspectives on the management of diffusion from the perspective of public policy:

1. Slow diffusion of innovation through different adopter categories-a process whereby different segments of a social system adopt an innovation at different points in time for different reasons.
2. Rapid diffusion through a moss market - diffusion of an innovation to the majority of a mass market by lowering perceived risk and change in habit to all members of a social system.
3. Diffusion in a competitive and regulated marketplace - diffusion, in which a monopolistic or a competitive situation exists, allowing greater or lesser innovation.
4. Diffusion in an environment which is technologically enabling-diffusion in an environment which has the technical infrastructure that is supportive of the innovation.

The traditional approach in marketing has been to view diffusion as a communication process and as a problem of appropriately targeting individual consumer segments (adopter categories). This approach is, perhaps, appropriate if indeed the different adopter segments have different needs and will adopt an innovation at different points in time. Such an approach might be appropriate to public policy makers (whether government or industry) if it is desirable that the diffusion of a product or idea is to be slow and controlled.

An alternative perspective that could be suggested by Sheth's (1981) LDC is that a majority of prospective adopters might all have the same reasons for initially resisting the innovation. If a common point of resistance with regard to perceived risk and change in habit can be found, then perhaps an innovation can be enhanced by launching an innovation which appeals to the majority of members of a social system rather than merely appealing to the "innovator"

10 Ownen, Robert et.al, "Public policy and diffusion of innovation", SOCIAL INDICATORS RESEARCH, 60(1-3), 2002(December):179-189

segment of adopters. In retrospect this appears to have worked to enable the diffusion of the automobile.

Asthana, Sheena et.al (2002)[11] has observed that as more and more staff is required to work in partnership, redefining the nature of their jobs and the boundaries of their percent organizations, information on the characteristics of effective partnerships becomes an increasingly salient resource. The evaluation of the HAZ programmes has not just on assessing the value of service reconfiguration and delivery but, just as importantly, on assessing the allied changes to organizational and individual work practice and ethos and ensuring that the learning from this change is disseminated. No framework for evaluation is intended to be a model of reality rather a tool that facilitates clear thinking. This paper has shown how such a tool can help dissect the complexity that is partnership working and provide assistance for strategic and operational staff alike in understanding the systems of which they are a part and the factors which inhibit or facilitate change. The MRAC model can grow from its already extensive coverage (more than 78000 members in almost 1750 groups in 925 separate villages in 1983, according to its 1983 repost BRAC 1983) to become a major force for promoting social change in Bangladesh as a whole (over 15 million house holds in 65000 villages counted in the 1981 census) remains to be seen. And whether the Upazila program (assuming that president Ershad goes ahead with its implementation) will be allowed to stay in place long enough for any social change to begin to percolate up through it also remains to be seen. But the BRAC experience indicates that social consciousness can be raised and can in a self directed manner mobilized it self, and the Indian Panchayat raj experience shows that if participatory structures of local self government are left in place for long enough, they can become instrumental in the social transformation that must take place in the rural majority its to have a say in managing its own future.

11 Asthana, Sheena et.al. "Partnership working in public policy provision: A framework for evaluation", SOCIAL POLICY AND ADMINISTRATION, 36(7), 2002(December):780-795

Mackie, Robert (2004)[12] this study examines public policy in relation to management development in Scottish local government over a 35-year period. Public policy implementation proliferated and theorists derived conclusions from these studies in the hope of preventing failure. The result was better informed policy but implementation problems still cannot be avoided by prospective, anticipatory policy design. There remains a need for policy formulators and implementers to have a capacity to learn and adapt to changing circumstances. Policy formulators and implementers have to ensure that policies 'fit' environmental circumstances thus avoiding a 'policy drift' between the policy and a changing public management environment. Studies of public policy and its implementation can therefore both inform policy formulation and enhance the capacity of implementers to adapt implementation to accommodate changing circumstances. The changing nature of public management over the last 20 years. Local government managers, especially at senior levels, are being bombarded with generic management development under the headings of strategic management and performance management but they are not being developed as public policy analysts and therefore lack fundamental knowledge and understanding of the public policy process. For some, therefore, the balance has shifted too far in favour of the generic, business' management competences to the disadvantage of the centrally important public management competences. Some public managers do not recognize the need to do well while doing well. At the author's own institution there remains a public management module on 'Decision-making for Policy and Strategy' that combines policy analysis with strategic public management. Public managers are not managers of a business. They can be businesslike, but policy is not strategy. Public managers implement policy while promoting the strategic and operational effectiveness of their employing organizations.

---

12 Mackie. Robert, "Local government management development in Scotland: A study of public policy and its implementation", 1967-02.LOCAL GOVERNMENT STUDIES, 30(3), 2004(Autumn): 345-359

Sharms, Vijay Paul (2013)[13] has noted that India's food subsidy system has been a major component of the social safety net for the poor, guaranteeing the availability of food grains at affordable price, helping to reduce malnutrition and ensuring price stability in the country. The results highlighted a number of issues in the food subsidy debate. The results show that food that the food subsidy has grown very sharply in the post-reforms period (from Rs. 4333 crore in Period I to Rs. 49070 crore in period IV), in fact, by more than 300 per cent in a period of just 6 years between 2006-07 and 2011-12. The food subsidy as a percentage of total GDP and agricultural GDP has also increased over the years (from 2.1 per cent of agricultural GDP in period I to 5.3 per cent in Period IV). The share of buffer subsidy has declined while the share of consumer subsidy has increased during the period. The rising economic cost, mainly due to increase in procurement prices, high procurement and off take of food grains and constant central issue price has been mainly responsible for increase in food subsidy. For example' procurement prices of rice and wheat have increased at an annual compound growth rate of about 11 percent during 2006-07 and 2011-12 and this had led to significant increase in economic cost of rice from Rs.1391 per quintal in 2006-07 to Rs.2184 in 2011-12 and wheat from Rs. 1178 to Rs. 1652. Procurement incidentals, another important component of subsidy have increased by about 6 percent in rice and over 11 percent in case of wheat. Under procurement costs, the component that contributed the most to food subsidy was statutory charges like many charges and purchase/sales tax VAT, which vary from less than 2 percent in some states to 14.5 percent in states like Punjab. Government intervention in the form of procurement should be selective and quantity of procurement should not exceed average annual off take at procurement price equal to cost C2 and amount of production where average farm harvest prices fall below cost A2 plus cost of family labour.

13 Sharms, Vijay Paul, "Food subsidy in India: Its components, Trends, causes and reforms for public policy", INDIAN JOURNAL OF AGRICULTURAL ECONOMICS, 68(2), 2013 (April-June): 195-221

Ifeyori, I and Ihimodu (2006)[14] have examined that the nature, characteristics and importance of rural infrastructures to the development of the rural areas and the economy in general. The need to maintain rural infrastructures has also been established. The two cases presented appeared to have highlighted the factors that could inhibit the maintenance of infrastructural facilities in the rural areas. These factors would seem to have emanated from the ways the facilities were created in the first place, which is an aspect of public policy. It, therefore, appears that public policy could influence people's decision either to, or not support or maintain rural infrastructures. And also summarizes the factors that should be promoted in order to encourage beneficiaries of rural facilities to create or imbibe the culture of maintenance of rural infrastructure.

Forbes, Kathyrn (2008)[15] has observed that the failure of the WHEN project illustrates how zoning policy may be used to prohibit or deter affordable housing projects. As Mendez (2O02:10) writes, "(such practices disproportionately affect Mexican Families across the state and only intensify the obstacles they encounter in achieving homeownership". In addition, Fresno County's response to the project brings to light ideologies about appropriate land use and representations of farm worker populations combine to rationalize the lack of government responsiveness to the lack of affordable housing. From the country's perspective, the lack of affordable housing stock is the result not of government policies but of an enduring failure in the low-income population. Fresno County, therefore, does not have the responsibility to meet the needs of its Mexican farm worker residents who are the backbone of the region's agriculture industry. The WHEN case study also brings to light how state and federal policy objectives initiated through funding streams

---

14 Ifeyori, I and Ihimodu, "Public policy and maintenance of rural infrastructure in Nigeria", AFRO-ASIAN JOURNAL OF RURAL DEVELOPMENT, 39(2), 2006(July-December): 65-74

15 Forbes, Kathyrn, "Bureaucratic strategies of exclusion: Land use ideology and images of Mexican farm workers in housing policy", HUMAN ORGANIZATION, 60(2), 2008(Summer): 196-209

targeted at the development of affordable housing may be thwarted by regionally specific goals and erroneous information. This is not to say that developing affordable housing for Mexican farm workers is impossible in Fresno County. It is to say that new advocacy strategies are necessary. First, affordable housing advocates need to engage in long-term education projects with policy makers in the region. Whereas policy makers at the state level readily consult policy institutes and advocacy groups to inform their decisions, local-level bureaucrats, at least in Fresno, do not. Affordable housing advocates need to develop policy centers that advice on regionally specific social issues set in a statewide and national context. And advocates need to create long-term relationships with county personnel outside of particular projects. It may be that WHEN failed, in part, because the county had not before considered that the Mexican farm worker population is heterogeneous, and that some sectors of the population are capable of purchasing subsidized or non subsidized homes. Through ongoing education, county personnel may gain a better understanding of the farm worker population and the issues it faces.

Second, county personnel need to be educated about how other agricultural and nonagricultural counties are increasing their supply of affordable housing. Currently, one-fifth of all cities and counties in California have adopted inclusionary zoning practices which are designed to increase the stock of affordable housing. Practices such as requiring developers to designate a percentage of new home construction to affordable housing projects and charging developer fees that are put into a local affordable housing fund are but two examples of inclusionary zoning practices. Much of the time, these practices are included in the general plan for a county. Unfortunately, not only has Fresno County failed to adopt such practices, many officials have the attitude that it is impossible to make developers build affordable housing. As one county supervisor said, "we have no way of making developers build houses or businesses commit to an area. The market determines what they will do".

Third, affordable housing advocates need to find a way to get involved in the development of general plans that direct a country's development rather than attempting to change the zoning policies after they have been adopted. The WHEN case study illustrates just how committed policy makers may be to the policies they themselves developed.

Finally, better education may not result in a local governmental commitment to increase the supply of affordable housing. Litigation may be the only way to force local governments to serve all of their constituents, not just those who are weai6. But litigation is not only a costly process but a lengthy one as well.

These strategies point to the importance of training anthropologists to work in public policy arenas. Anthropology departments increasingly are incorporating policy research and advocacy into their graduate programs. This policy training includes teaching anthropologists how to communicate their information to lay audiences and how to strategically deploy this information to meet specific goals.

Mohanty, Bidyut[16] has observed that NREGS has not been able to help in deepening grassroots democracy or strengthening the PRIs even though the scheme has brought about some positive impact on the beneficiaries. The members of local government lack knowledge about micro planning, social audit, vigilance committees etc since they don't have functionaries of their own. In order to make the decentralized decision-making process a reality, the NREGS should be implemented through the panchayats by proper devolution and without having any undue interference from the block and district.

Datar, Chhaya[17] has found that the NREGS has not yet picked up momentum because government machinery is paralyzed. In the present circumstances, the NREGS would acquire life only if there is a groundswell of the poor willing to pressurize the administration.

---

16 Mohanty, Bidyut, Working of NREGA---Voices from Panchayats, MAINSTREAM, 57(15), 2009(March): 25-28

17 Datar, Chhaya, Failure of national rural employment guarantee scheme in Maharashtra, ECONOMIC AND POLITICAL WEEKLY, 42(34), 2007(August): 3454-3459

Saklani, Joginder Singh[18] has opined that NREGS has the potential to lead to the empowerment of the poor people and usher in greater democratization if the opportunity thrown up by the scheme is put to effective use. Careful identification of assets to be created is necessary to ensure that they are capable of having multiplier effects on the rural economy. The extent of mobilization and awareness building, as well as conflict that emerges in its implementation will determine the success of MNREGS.

Khera, Reetika[19] has analyzed the experience of the Jagrut Adivasi Dalit Sangathan in Madhya Pradesh and shows the power of grassroots organizational work in activating the National Rural Employment Guarantee Scheme. Levels of NREGS employment in the Sangathan areas are found to be as high as 85 days per household per year, and nearly half of all working households have got 100 days of work. They also earned the minimum wage. The act is considered to be an opportunity to promote overall rural development and alter the balance of power in village society.

Venkataiah, C[20] has opined that right to work through MGNREGS involves not only the provision of employment to every person, able and willing to work; but also that the employment provided is gainful, contributing enough to provide maintenance to workers in all circumstances. The policies relating to right to work should also aim at ensuring that the work provided is as productive as possible in safeguarding the fundamental economic and political freedoms of an individual; there should be freedom of choice of employment and fullest possible opportunity for each worker qualify for and to use his/her skills and endowments, in a job work for which he/she is well suited.

---

18 Saklani, Joginder Singh, Implementation of National Rural Employment Guarantee Scheme: a study of Mandi District in Himachal Pradesh. MAN AND DEVELOPMENT, 34(2), 2012(June): 25-40

19 Khera, Reetika, Empowerment guarantee act. ECONOMIC AND POLITICAL WEEKLY, 43(35), 2008(October): 8-10

20 Venkataiah, C Inclusive growth strategy: a study of NREGS in Andhra Pradesh. INDIAN JOURNAL OF PUBLIC ADMINISTRATION, 54(4), 2008 (October-Decem): 850-865

Das, Vidhya and Pradhan, Pramod[21] have observed that despite impressive achievements, there is shocking invisibility of the said achievements on the ground. More than this non delivery is the connivance in corruption that appears to prevail from top to bottom. There is a complete disregard for any form of accountability, and people's complaints and appeals are ignored again and again. The government has taken several progressive steps but, it should not sit back and count its laurels.

Dutta, Puja et.al[22] have observed that participation rates on the scheme are higher for poor people than others. This holds at the official poverty line, but the scheme is also reaching many families just above the official line. It is only at relatively high consumption levels that participation drops off sharply. This should not be interpreted as indication that well-off families in rural India are turning to MGNREGS.

Siddhartha and Vanaik, Anish[23] have analyzed the CAG report with reference to MGNREGS. They have observed that the CAG report has highlighted many genuine problems and pointed out improvements that are required. Even the limited experience of conditions on the ground has yielded a fairly rich harvest of recommendations. Much of findings need translation in to "policies and programmes". It is pointed out that the exaggerated claims of the media and the fact that questions are being raised about the Act itself, has led the government to go in to denial mode. For the government to simply issue rebuttals and bury its head in the sand about the fact that many of the things necessary for effective implementation have not been put in to place.

---

21 Das, Vidhya and Pradhan, Pramod, Illusions of change
ECONOMIC AND POLITICAL WEEKLY, 42(32), 2007(August): 3283-3287

22 Dutta, Puja et.al, Does India's employment Guarantee Scheme Guarantee Employment.
ECONOMIC AND POLITICAL WEEKLY, 47(16), 2012(April): 55-64

23 Siddhartha and Vanaik, Anish, CAG Report on NREGA: Fact and fiction.
ECONOMIC AND POLITICAL WEEKLY, 43(25), 2008(June): 39-45

Khera, Reetika et.al[24] have opined that for effective participation by women, it is important for the NREGS to go beyond the initial gender-related provisions such as fixing the minimum share of women workers and equal wages. A more comprehensive perspective on gender equality needs to be built in all aspects of the Act. They felt that one of the first steps in this direction is to move from the household entitlement of 100 days to individual entitlements, which will assure women 100 days of work in their own right, without having to negotiate within the household. In order to ensure direct access to NREGS earnings, instead of having joint bank accounts, there should be separate bank accounts for women. This has already been done in some states (e g, in Tamil Nadu, men and women have separate job cards and separate bank accounts). It is suggested that increasing the share of women in NREGS staff appointments would also go a long way towards achieving the agenda of gender equality and sensitivity.

Ambasta, Pramathesh[25] has observed that the NREGS ranks among the most powerful initiatives ever undertaken for transformation of rural livelihoods in India. The unprecedented commitment of financial resources is matched only by its imaginative architecture that promises a radically fresh programme of rural development. However, for NREGS to realise its potential, it must focus on raising the productivity of agriculture in India's most backward regions. This can then lead further to the creation of allied livelihoods on the foundation of water security. This is also the only way we can envision a decline in the size of the work guarantee over time, as public investment under NREGS leads to higher rural incomes, that in turn, spurs private investment and greater incomes and employment.

---

24 Khera, Reetika et.al, Women workers and perceptions of the National Rural Employment Guarantee Act,
ECONOMIC AND POLITICAL WEEKLY, 45(43), 2009(October): 49-57

25 Ambasta, Pramathesh, Two years of NREGA: The road ahead.
ECONOMIC AND POLITICAL WEEKLY, 43(8), 2008(February): 41-50

Dey, Subhasish[26] has found that there is universal awareness about the NREGS, job cards have been made available to all those who have applied and NREGS-related information is well-maintained and relatively accessible. While there were long delays in wage payments during the first year of the programme, since then, the payment lag has declined and it is now in the range of 20 days. While this delay is not consistent with the provisions of the Act, it is a clear improvement from the 42-day lag observed in the first year. Notwithstanding these positive aspects, with respect to one of the main goals of the Act, that is, the provision of work when alternative employment opportunities are scarce, the NREGS is not fulfilling its role. There is a need for an innovative thinking on how to use the available resources to create jobs and construct useful rural infrastructure.

Ashok Pankaj and Rukmini Tankha[27] have opined that empowerment of rural women has emerged as an unintended consequence of MGNREGS women have benefited more as workers than as a community. Women as individuals have gained because of their ability to earn independently, made possible due to the paid employment opportunity under MGNREGS. Independent and monetized earnings have increased consumption choices and reduced economic dependence. This has helped women in registering their tangible contribution to the household's income. The overall effects of these have translated in to increased safer women in household affairs.

ASPECTS COVERED IN THE EARLIER STUDIES

- The ways and means through which MGNREGS can be made effective
- The organization of poor required for the success of MGNREGS

26 Dey, Subhasish. National rural employment guarantee scheme in Birbhum. ECONOMIC AND POLITICAL WEEKLY, 45(41), 2010(October): 19-24

27 Ashok Pankaj and Rukmini Tankha, "Empowerment effects of the NREGS on women workers: a study in four states", Economic and Political Weekly, July 24, 2010, VOL.XLV, No.30, pp 45-55

- Empowerment of the poor
- Implications of MGNREGS on living standerds
- The role NGOs in MGNREGS implementation
- Right to work ensured through MGNREGS
- Rampant corruption in MGNREGS
- Low participation rates in MGNREGS
- CAG reports on MGNREGS
- From household entitlement to individual entitlement of employment
- The potentialities of MGNREGS
- Awareness about MGNREGS
- Asset creation through MGNREGS

GAPS IN THE EARLIER STUDIES

1. The impact of MGNREGS on the political processes of a village is not properly appreciated.
2. Employment and income variations attributable to MGNREGS (marginal effects) among the beneficiaries are not apprised properly.
3. The gap analysis between the expectations from and achievements of MGNREGS.

Chapter-3

SOCIO-ECONOMIC PROFILE OF THE BENEFICIARIES OF MGNREGS

An attempt is made in this chapter to discuss the profile of Nalgonda district and also discussed the socio-economic profile of the beneficiaries of the MGNREGS, in Nalgonda district. The present chapter is divided into two sections namely section-A and section-B. Section-A deals with the profile of Nalgonda district. Section-B deals with the socio-economic profile of the beneficiaries of the MGNREGS programs in the study area.

SECTION-A

Nalgonda district covers an area of 14,22,000 ha of which only 5.6% of the area is under forests, 7.8% is put to non-agricultural uses, 4.3% under pasture and 21.2% under current fallows. The net sown area accounts for 33.6% of the geographical area and the cropping intensity is 117%. The total population of the district is 32, 47,982 of which Scheduled Castes constitute 5,75,788 (17.73%), thus, accounting for the highest SC population both in percent and absolute numbers within NAIP districts. Scheduled Tribe population accounts for 10.55%. Nalgonda has the highest number of rural literates (67.6%) next only to Khammam and Warangal. Agricultural labourers represent 42% of the population while cultivators represent 25.5%. Percentage of workers engaged in non-agricultural activities is 32.4. Buffaloes (5, 92,271) outnumber cattle (5, 15,852) in this district while sheep and goats are numbered at 4,45,184. Thus, Nalgonda ranks third among the NAIP districts to have the largest number of adult cattle units (15,53,307). The grazing pressure is accounted at 6.3 ACU/ha grazing area, which is the lowest among NAIP districts. The normal annual rainfall of the district is 744 mm with a very high frequency of droughts during the past 15 years. The district has 1,87,000 ha of net irrigated area accounting for 36% of the total cultivated area. In the past 10 years, rice, castor, and groundnut have lost considerable area while cotton, green gram and pigeon pea have gained substantially. Despite this, rice continues to occupy 1/3rd of the cropped area. The productivity of castor and cotton during TE-2005 is 326 and 220 kg/ha, respectively. On the other hand, the average yield of rice is relatively higher at 2688 kg/ha. This district has seen a tremendous increase in area under horticulture crops. From a mere 17,000 ha in 2000-01, it has increased to over 71,000 ha in 2005-06 contributing to over 10% of the area under horticulture in the State. The area under vegetables has increased slightly from 3,377 ha to 5,358 ha and that under spices has marginally decreased during the period. Nalgonda district had a per capita income of Rs. 16526 during 2003-04. The annual growth rate of agricultural lending was 30% in the district. Nalgonda has the highest number of APMCs (24) among the NAIP districts and has the second highest density of APMCs (5.1 per lakh ha of NSA) next only to Ranga Reddy district.

INDIRAMMA

(Integrated Novel Development in Rural Areas and Model Municipal Areas)

Hon. Ex-Chief Minister of Andhra Pradesh Dr. Y.S. RajSekhar Reddy launched the historic INDIRAMMA programme to create a novel rural/urban Andhra Pradesh through the development of villages and municipalities in an integrated manner

Governments have been implementing many programmes over the years for the development of infrastructure and on individual welfare. Since there is always a universal aspiration of all the people to be part of this developmental process, the impact of the programmes implemented so far is not quite visible due to the scattered nature of the distribution of the resources. As of now, there is hardly any objective, equitable and verifiable criteria in the selection of towns and villages while implementing the programmes. An ad-hoc allocation of money for various programmes has come into vogue instead of using the village as a unit for integrated planning. Even while sanctioning programmes and welfare measures all the genuine requirements of the villages/towns are not being considered, resulting in avoidable dissatisfaction among the public. Thus the approach is open-ended and not focused.

Keeping the above in view, Andhra Pradesh Government has taken a decision to take up development of model villages and towns with an intention to saturate certain identified basic needs of the people and the village/town Infrastructure In an integrated and focused manner. This is planned to be achieved in a period of three years.

This new model of development is named as **"INDIRAMMA"** (Integrated Novel Development in Rural Areas & Model Municipal Areas) to fulfill the dreams of our former Prime Minister, Smt. Indira Gandhi. The objective of this programme is to saturate the basic needs in respect of the identified activities in all the Villages and Towns over a period of Three years. Such a development model will ensure the overall development of the Villages/Towns in a transparent manner covering additional areas every year. This process will remove the uncertainty and skepticism in certain quarters with regard to coverage of all eligible beneficiaries and the infrastructure needs since all the villages/towns are covered over a period of three years. The primary aim of this programme is to provide in every village Pucca houses, drinking water supply, individual sanitary latrines, drainage, power supply to every household, Road facilities for transport, pensions to eligible old age persons, weavers, widows and the disabled, primary education to all, special nutrition to adolescent girls/pregnant and lactating women and better health facilities in all the villages over a period of three years in a saturation mode, This shall improve the living standards of the people significantly.

This programme will be taken up in all the mandals simultaneously. Taking up Gram Panchayats covering one-third of the population in the manadal every year, all the Gram Panchayats will be covered over a period of three years. 8026 Gram Panchayats have been selected for the first phase of the programme starting on 1st April 2006 and the remaining Gram Panchayats will be covered during the subsequent two years. Government is ready to launch the programme from 1st April 2006 and Gram Sabhas will be held in the selected Gram Panchayats from 6th February 2006 to give details of the specific activities to be taken up in the village under the programme.

In Nalgonda, district Self Help Groups have been formed in the name of "SAMABHAVANA" in the year 1995. The SAMABHAVANA considering

SA - Sanchayika (Savings)
MA - Mahilabhyudaya (Women Development)
BHA - Bhavi Pourula Abhivrudhi (Children Development)
VA - Vana Samarakshana (Afforestation)
NA - Nadi Parivahaka Prantha Abhivrudi (Development through Watershed)

The SAMABHAVANA groups have been formed with 10-15 women members with a daily savings of Rs. 2/- each from their earnings. The groups themselves are doing internal lending from their savings to needy women in the group with simple interest. This amount can be utilized for doing agriculture, medical expenditure & children education etc. In this way, group savings have been increased and as well as family financial problems solved without going for outside lending with a higher rate of interest.

The groups which were completed one year period and more than 10,000 savings will be provided with matching grant, subsidy, and Bank loans Sanitary Napkins under SGSY in the name of "SWETCHA MAHILA". The sanitary napkins production has been taken up to popularize the utilization among the rural women for improving the Health and Hygienic conditions. These products are made available at reasonable prices within the reach of poor women.

Minor Irrigation

Nearly 59051 SCs were covered under minor irrigation programmes, by taking up minor irrigation sources and allied activities like Bore Wells, open wells, Dug - cum - Bore wells, Filter Points, Electric Motors, Lift irrigation schemes etc., and spent an amount of Rs. 3686 lakhs through this society in various manuals.

Successful initiatives in Nalgonda district

The following were the successful initiatives taken up during the year 2001-2002 in Nalgonda district

(*A*) Convergence of self-employment schemes through integrated action plan:

The following 9 developmental departments were brought under an integrated action plan 2001-02. District Rural Development Agency (DRDA), Scheduled Castes (SC) Corporation, Backward Class (BC) Corporation, Modified Area Development Agency (MADA), Minorities, Youth Welfare, Women Development and Child Welfare, Khadi Village and Industries Board (K.V.I.B). Implementation of this action plan has been divided into 9 stages.

I: Selection of Villages: As it is not possible to cover all the villages in one financial year, all the villages in the mandal have been divided into 5 parts with a view to cover all the villages in a span of 5 years. 1/5 the of the villages which are so far not covered or least covered were selected.

II: Gramasabhas and identification of beneficiaries: In the selected villages Gramasabhas were conducted @ one gramasabha per day. Beneficiaries pertaining to all the developmental departments were identified in the gram sabha as per the targets. The gramasabha was presided by the sarpanch and elected representatives like Mandal Praja Parishad (MPP), Mandal Parishad Territorial Candidate (MPTC), Zilla Parishad Territorial Candidate (ZPTC), Member of Legislative Assembly (MLAs) etc have attended and from officers' side Mandal Revenue Officer (MRO), Mandal Parishad Development Officer (MPDO), Village

Development Officer (VDO), Village Administrative Officer (VAO) and bankers have attended.

III: Awareness camps and Entrepreneur Development Programmes: For all the selected beneficiaries' awareness programmes were conducted at the erstwhile block level and cost economics were furnished on various schemes in order to facilitate the beneficiary to select the suitable scheme.

Stage - IV: Documentation: All the selected beneficiaries were called to respective MPDO offices for undertaking documentation on a single day. All the concerned officers were asked to be available at the MPDO office to issue relevant certificates to complete the documentation. This will avoid repeated visits by the beneficiary to various government offices at the cost of his time and money.

Stage - V: Sanctions: After completion of the documentation the MPDOs have submitted proposals to the district offices. Sanctions were accorded and orders were sent to all the concerned.

Stage - VI: Training: During this stage training to all the beneficiaries on how to carry out the selected economic activities was being imparted.

Stage - VII: Grounding of units: Grounding of units were done by the banker. The subsidy and margin money was placed at disposal of the banker.

Stage - VIII: Asset verification: To guide the beneficiary on the management of the asset and to avoid any misutilization, inspections were undertaken by the officers to verify the assets.

Stage - IX: Loan recovery drive: A joint loan recovery drive by the nodal team and banker has been contemplated to affect the recovery of the loans.

(*B*) Policy initiatives

(i) Entrustment of Civil works to SHGs three-fourth Execution of civil works were entrusted to SHGs third-fourth SHGs were given necessary technical training on the execution of works and they were provided detail booklets. ¾ About 562 works worth Rs. 376.00 lakhs were entrusted from Panchayat Raj Department to the self-help groups third-fourth In the same way, Roads and Buildings department entrusted 20 works worth of Rs. 3.29 lakhs and Irrigation department entrusted 3 works worth of Rs. 3.70 lakhs to the self-help groups

(ii) Supplies to welfare hostels entrusted to SHGs

Three-fourth All the welfare hostel supplies like provisions and commodities were entrusted to SHGs. Three-fourth

- The SHGs were conducting out the business worth of 27.16 lakhs per month towards supplies to the SC, ST and BC welfare hostels and were generating an income of Rs. 3.00 lakhs per month.

(iii) Raising of nurseries was entrusted to SHGs:

- Three-fourth 68 groups raised about 40 lakhs plants and earned appropriately Rs. 9000/- per group/season

(iv) Fair price shops were entrusted to SHGs:

- Three-fourth of 140 appointments were issued to SHGs to run fair price shops

(v) Punt service contract was entrusted to SHGs:

- Three-fourth at Mattampally on river Krishna 3 groups are managing and earning 1.5 lakhs per year by providing punt services i.e. carrying passengers from Nalgonda district side to Guntur district side across the river.

(vi) Non-Timber Forest Produce – contracts were entrusted to SHGs:

- Three-fourth In 7 mandals 21 groups collected NTFP and earned Rs. 5000/- per group in a season. Eg. Custard apple

(*C*) Other income generating activities

(i) SHGs managing HLL rural distributorship:

- Three-fourth Five Mutually Aided Cooperative and Thrift (MACT) Societies distributed HLL products to entire Nalgonda district covering rural retailers and SANGHA MITRA super bazaars were managed by 10 MACT Societies. The profit margin was about 13%.

(ii) Family Welfare:

(iii) Cement bricks:

Three-fourth of 69 SHGs took up manufacturing of cement solid bricks and sold to DM (Housing) through NIRMITHI KENDRAs.

(iv) Super bazaars:

Three-fourth of 10 MACT Societies started income generating activity under SANGHA MITRA super bazaars. Each unit was established with an outlay of Rs. 2.00 lakhs. The profit margin was 10% i.e. Rs. 4000/- to 5000/- per month.

(v) Sanitary Napkins:

- Three-fourth of to improve health and hygiene of rural women sanitary napkin units were established with an outlay of Rs. 7.00 lakhs. The product was sold at a profit of Rs. 5/- per pack under the brand name "SWETCHA MAHILA".

(vi) Wealth from the waste:

Three-fourth of 9 charcoal units were established in 9 mandals with an outlay of Rs. 1.00 lakh by using prosophis species and they earned Rs. 5000/- per 10 Mt.

(vii) Land Lease:

- Three-fourth of 15 groups have taken about 100 acres of land on lease and raised vegetables, commercial crops etc

SECTION-B

An attempt is made in this section to discuss various parameters of socio-economic development which include

- Place
- Gender
- Age of the respondents
- Social status
- Type of the family
- Occupation
- Education

Table-3.1: Place

place	Frequency	Percent	Cumulative Percent
palavaram	40	20.0	20.0
Pedda Ravulapally	40	20.0	40.0
Goodapoor	40	20.0	60.0
Mallaprajpally	40	20.0	80.0
Chirumarthy	40	20.0	100.0
Total	200	100.0	

Source: primary data

Table-3.1 refers to the distribution of the beneficiaries of the MGNREGP by their place. It is observed that 40 beneficiary respondents from each sample village are selected. Thus, 40 beneficiary respondents covered under MGNREGS Palavaram, 40 from Peddaravulapally, 40 from Goodapur, 40 from Mallaprajpally, and 40 from Chirumarthy village are selected.

Table-3.2: Gender

Gender	Frequency	Percent	Cumulative Percent
Male	138	69.0	69.0
Female	62	31.0	100.0
Total	200	100.0	

Source: primary data

Table-3.2 refers to the distribution of the beneficiaries of the MGNREGS by their gender. It is observed that 69 percent of the sample beneficiary respondents are male and 31 percent are female.

Table-3.3: Age of the respondents

(Years)	Frequency	Percent	Cumulative Percent
20-30	53	26.5	26.5
30-45	117	58.5	85.0
Above 45	30	15.0	100.0
Total	200	100.0	

Source: primary data

Table-3.3 refers to the distribution of the beneficiaries of the MGNREGS by their age. It is observed that 26.5 percent of the sample beneficiary respondents are from the age range of 20-30 years, followed by 58.5 percent from 30-45 years and 15 percent are from above 45 years range. Thus, the majority of the sample beneficiary respondents are found to be relatively young.

Table-3.4: Social status

	Frequency	Percent	Cumulative Percent
OC	22	11.0	11.0
BC	96	48.0	59.0
SC	38	19.0	78.0
ST	28	14.0	92.0
Others	16	8.0	100.0
Total	200	100.0	

Source: primary data

Table-3.4 refers to the distribution of the beneficiaries of the MGNREGS by their social status. It is observed that 11 percent of the sample beneficiary respondents are drawn from socially advanced castes, followed by 48 percent are from backward castes, 19 percent are from scheduled castes, 14 percent are from scheduled tribes and 8 percent are from another category. Thus, the majority of the sample beneficiary respondents are drawn from socially downtrodden communities.

Table-3.5: Type of the family

Type of the family	Frequency	Percent	Cumulative Percent
Joint	54	27.0	27.0
Nuclear	146	73.0	100.0
Total	200	100.0	

Source: primary data

Table-3.5 refers to the distribution of the beneficiaries of the MGNREGS by their type of family. It is observed that 27 percent of the sample beneficiary respondents are drawn from the joint family system and 73 percent are from nuclear families.

Table-3.6: Occupation

Occupation	Frequency	Percent	Cumulative Percent
Agriculture	58	29.0	29.0
Caste based	142	71.0	100.0
Total	200	100.0	

Source: primary data

Table-3.6 refers to the distribution of the beneficiaries of the MGNREGS by their occupation. It is observed that 29 percent of the sample beneficiary respondents are with agriculture as their occupation and 71 percent of the respondents from caste-based occupations. Thus, the sample composition is predominant with caste-based occupations.

Table-3.7: Education

Education	Frequency	Percent	Cumulative Percent
Illiterate	57	28.5	28.5
Literate	143	71.5	100.0
Total	200	100.0	

Source: primary data

Table-3.7 refers to the distribution of the beneficiaries of the MGNREGS by their education. It is observed that 28.5 percent of the sample beneficiary respondents are illiterates and 71.5 percent of the respondents are found to be literates.

Table-3.8: Type of the house

Education	Frequency	Percent	Cumulative Percent
Nil	26	13	13
Kutcha	54	27	40
Semi Pucca	48	24	64
Pucca	72	36	100
Total	200	100.0	

Source: primary data

Table-3.8 refers to the distribution of the beneficiaries of the MGNREGS by the type of the owned house. It is observed that 13 percent of the sample beneficiary respondents did not own a house, 27 percent of the respondents owned kutcha houses, 24 percent of the respondents owned semi pucca houses, and 36 percent of the respondents owned pucca houses in the study area.

Table-3.9: Do you receive the pension

Response	Frequency	Percent	Cumulative Percent
Yes	45	22.5	22.5
No	155	77.5	100.0
Total	200	100.0	

Source: primary data

Table-3.9 refers to the distribution of the beneficiaries of the MGNREGS by their response about the receipt of a pension. It is observed that 22.5 percent of the sample beneficiary respondents have received old age pension and widow pensions and 77.5 percent of the respondents did not receive the pension.

Table-3.10: Are you a member of Self Help Group?

Response	Frequency	Percent	Cumulative Percent
Yes	62	31	31
No	138	69	100.0
Total	200	100.0	

Source: primary data

Table-3.10 refers to the distribution of the beneficiaries of the MGNREGS by their response about the membership in self-help groups. It is observed that 31 percent of the sample beneficiary respondents have become the member of self-help groups and 69 percent of the respondents did not become members of SHGs.

Table-3.11: Have you received house site patta from the government?

Response	Frequency	Percent	Cumulative Percent
Yes	135	67.5	67.5
No	65	32.5	100.0
Total	200	100.0	

Source: primary data

Table-3.11 refers to the distribution of the beneficiaries of the MGNREGS by their response about the receipt of house site patta from the government. It is observed that 67.5 percent of the sample beneficiary respondents have received house site patta from government and 32.5 percent of the respondents did not receive the same.

Table-3.12: Are you the beneficiary of Indira Aavas Yojana?

Response	Frequency	Percent	Cumulative Percent
Yes	200	100	100
No	0.00	0.00	100.0
Total	200	100.0	

Source: primary data

Table-3.12 refers to the distribution of the beneficiaries of the MGNREGS by their response about whether they are the beneficiaries of the IAY scheme. It is observed that all 100 percent of the sample beneficiary respondents have received house under IAY scheme.

Table-3.13: Availability of infrastructure- School

Response	Frequency	Percent	Cumulative Percent
Yes	200	100	100
No	0	0.00	100.0
Total	200	100.0	

Source: primary data

Table-3.13 refers to the distribution of the beneficiaries of the MGNREGS by their response about the availability of infrastructure namely school and road in the colony where they stay and which is sanctioned under the IAY scheme. All the 100 percent sample respondents have the school and road facilities in the IAY colonies.

Table-3.14: Availability of infrastructure- Drinking water

Response	Frequency	Percent	Cumulative Percent
Yes	146	73	73
No	54	27	100.0
Total	200	100.0	

Source: primary data

Table-3.14 refers to the distribution of the beneficiaries of the MGNREGS by their response about the availability of infrastructure namely drinking water facility in the colony where they stay and which is sanctioned under the IAY scheme. It is observed that 73 percent sample respondents have the drinking water facilities in the IAY colonies and 27 percent of the respondents did not subscribe to this view.

Table-3.15: Availability of infrastructure- Roads

Response	Frequency	Percent	Cumulative Percent
Yes	126	63	63
No	74	37	100.0
Total	200	100.0	

Source: primary data

Table-3.15 refers to the distribution of the beneficiaries of the MGNREGS by their response about the availability of infrastructure namely road facility in the colony where they stay and which is sanctioned under IAY scheme. It is observed that 63 percent sample respondents have got the road facilities in the IAY colonies and 37 percent of the respondents did not subscribe to this view.

Table-3.16: Availability of infrastructure- Health facilities

Response	Frequency	Percent	Cumulative Percent
Yes	184	92	92
No	16	08	100.0
Total	200	100.0	

Source: primary data

Table-3.16 refers to the distribution of the beneficiaries of the MGNREGS by their response about the availability of infrastructure namely health facilities in the colony where they stay and which is sanctioned under the IAY scheme. It is observed that 92 percent sample respondents have got the health facilities in the IAY colonies and 08 percent of the respondents did not subscribe to this view.

Table-3.17: Availability of infrastructure-Anganwadi

Response	Frequency	Percent	Cumulative Percent
Yes	110	55	55
No	90	45	100.0
Total	200	100.0	

Source: primary data

Table-3.17 refers to the distribution of the beneficiaries of the MGNREGS by their response about the availability of infrastructure namely Anganwadi facilities in the colony where they stay and which is sanctioned under the IAY scheme. It is observed that 55 percent sample respondents have got the Anganwadi facilities in the IAY colonies and 45 percent of the respondents did not subscribe to this view.

Table-3.18: Availability of infrastructure-primary health center

Response	Frequency	Percent	Cumulative Percent
Yes	84	42	73
No	116	58	100.0
Total	200	100.0	

Source: primary data

Table-3.18 refers to the distribution of the beneficiaries of the MGNREGS by their response about the availability of infrastructure namely primary health center facilities in the colony where they stay and which is sanctioned under the IAY scheme. It is observed that 42 percent sample respondents have got the primary health center facilities in the IAY colonies and 58 percent of the respondents did not subscribe to this view.

Table-3.19: Impact of development schemes- Migration

Response	Frequency	Percent	Cumulative Percent
Low	150	75	75
Moderate	40	20	95
High	10	5	100
Total	200	100.0	

Source: primary data

Table-3.19 refers to the distribution of the beneficiaries of rural development programs with a focus on MGNREGS and its impact on migration. It is observed that 75 percent of the respondents have opined that the impact of rural development programs on migration is low and the same is moderate in the case of 20 percent of the respondents and high for 5 percent of the respondents.

Table-3.20: Impact of development schemes- social change

Response	Frequency	Percent	Cumulative Percent
Positive	130	65	65
Negative	60	30	95
Neutral	10	5	100
Total	200	100.0	

Source: primary data

Table-3.20 refers to the distribution of the beneficiaries of rural development programs with a focus on MGNREGS and its impact on social change. It is observed that 65 percent of the respondents have opined that the impact of rural development programs on social change is positive and the same is negative in the case of 30 percent of the respondents and neutral for 5 percent of the respondents.

Table-3.21: Impact of development schemes- cultural change

Response	Frequency	Percent	Cumulative Percent
Positive	100	50	50
Negative	40	20	70
Neutral	60	30	100
Total	200	100.00	

Source: primary data

Table-3.21 refers to the distribution of the beneficiaries of rural development programs with a focus on MGNREGS and its impact on cultural change. It is observed that 50 percent of the respondents have opined that the impact of rural development programs on cultural change is positive and the same is negative in the case of 20 percent of the respondents and neutral for 30 percent of the respondents.

Table-3.22: Impact of development schemes- educational change

Response	Frequency	Percent	Cumulative Percent
Positive	140	70	70
Negative	40	20	90
Neutral	20	10	100
Total	200	100.00	

Source: primary data

Table-3.22 refers to the distribution of the beneficiaries of rural development programs with a focus on MGNREGS and its impact on educational change. It is observed that 70 percent of the respondents have opined that the impact of rural development programs on educational change is positive and the same is negative in the case of 20 percent of the respondents and neutral for 10 percent of the respondents.

It is concluded that the beneficiaries of the MGNREGS are mostly male, relatively young, drawn from socially downtrodden castes, mostly from joint family systems and the majority are literates.

Chapter- 4

BENEFICIARY PERCEPTIONS OF PERFORMANCE OF MGNREGS

An attempt is made in this chapter to discuss the beneficiary perceptions of the performance of MGNREGS program, governance practices, political processes, challenges in the implementation of MGNREGS, expectations of the beneficiaries in the study area. The said parameters include

- Number of job cards
- Job cards through
- Days of employment
- Wage rate
- The time lag for getting the job
- Time lag to get the wage
- Sources of information
- Institution through which wages are provided
- Whether bank accounts opened
- Corruption for getting job cards
- The approach of employees towards MGNREGS
- Politicization of MGNREGS works
- Communalization of MGNREGS works
- The effectiveness of inspection of MGNREGS Works
- Awareness levels about 100 day's employment
- Awareness levels about minimum wages

- Awareness levels about equal wages
- Awareness levels about payment mode Awareness levels about stipulated % of women
- Awareness levels about treatment allowance
- Awareness levels about crèche
- Awareness levels about the tent for children
- Awareness levels about water Awareness levels about first aid
- Awareness levels about job card application
- Awareness levels about women inclusion policy of 33%
- Impact of MGNREGS on household's expenditure
- Impact of MGNREGS on migration
- Impact of MGNREGS on economic conditions
- Impact of MGNREGS on children education
- Impact of MGNREGS on changes in cultural life
- Impact of MGNREGS on absolute poverty
- Impact of MGNREGS on unemployment
- Whether the RTI act is effectively used
- Governance in MGNREGS- Efficiency
- Governance in MGNREGS-Effectiveness
- Governance in MGNREGS-Transparency
- Governance in MGNREGS-Responsiveness
- Governance in MGNREGS-inclusiveness
- Governance in MGNREGS-Accountability
- Governance in MGNREGS-Consensus-based decisions
- Governance in MGNREGS-Rule of law
- Governance in MGNREGS-Participation
- Governance in MGNREGS-Overall impact
- Political processes of MGNREGS -Frequency of Gram Sabha
- Political processes of MGNREGS -Participation in Gram Sabha
- Political processes of MGNREGS -Decision making at Gram Sabha

- Political processes of MGNREGS -Management of differences among the stakeholders in Gram Sabha
- Political processes of MGNREGS-Political bias
- Political processes of MGNREGS -Social neutrality
- Political processes of MGNREGS-Involvement of different political parties
- Challenges in the implementation of MGNREGS-Delay in releasing the grants
- Challenges in the implementation of MGNREGS-Predominance of political interests over development interests
- Challenges in the implementation of MGNREGS-Ambiguity in the composition of works
- Challenges in the implementation of MGNREGS-Lack of full support from the beneficiaries
- Challenges in the implementation of MGNREGS-Low convergence of the related programs
- Challenges in the implementation of MGNREGS-Failure to forge social capital
- Expectations-High wage rate
- Expectations-More man-days of employment
- Expectations-Measures to promote agri. business
- Expectations-Development of common property resources
- Expectations-Community agriculture works
- Expectations-Thorough social audit

Table-4.1: Number of job cards

	Frequency	Percent	Cumulative Percent
100	40	20.0	20.0
83	40	20.0	40.0
120	40	20.0	60.0

	Frequency	Percent	Cumulative Percent
69	40	20.0	80.0
87	40	20.0	100.0
Total	200	100.0	

Source: primary data

Table-4.1 refers to the distribution of the beneficiaries of the MGNREGS by the number of job cards. It is observed that the average job cards per family are 2.295.

Table-4.2: Job cards through

Job cards through	Frequency	Percent	Cumulative Percent
Gram Sabha	145	72.5	72.5
Village politician	30	15.0	87.5
Self awareness	25	12.5	100.0
Total	200	100.0	

Source: primary data

Table-4.2 refers to the distribution of the beneficiaries of the MGNREGS by the number of job cards. It is observed that 28.5 percent of the sample beneficiary respondents are illiterates and 71.5 percent of the respondents are found to be literates.

Table-4.3: Days of employment

Days of employment	Frequency	Percent	Cumulative Percent
40-60	59	29.5	29.5
60-80	115	57.5	87.0
Above 80	26	13.0	100.0
Total	200	100.0	

Source: primary data

Table-4.3 refers to the distribution of the beneficiaries of the MGNREGS by the days of employment. It is observed that 29.5

percent of the sample beneficiary respondents have got employment in the range of 40-60 man-days of employment under MGNREGS, and the same is 60-80 man-days of employment for 57.5 percent of the respondents and above 80 days of employment in the case of 13 percent of the respondents.

Table-4.4: Wage rate

Wage rate	Frequency	Percent	Cumulative Percent
70-80	31	15.5	15.5
80-90	122	61.0	76.5
Above 90	47	23.5	100.0
Total	200	100.0	

Source: primary data

Table-4.4 refers to the distribution of the beneficiaries of the MGNREGS by the wage rate. It is observed that 15.5 percent of the sample beneficiary respondents have got wage rate in the range of 70-80 rupees under MGNREGS, and the same is 80-90 rupees for 61 percent of the respondents and above 90 rupees in the case of 23.5 percent of the respondents.

Table-4.5: The time lag for getting the job

The time lag for getting the job	Frequency	Percent	Cumulative Percent
Up to 15 days	74	37.0	37.0
Above 15 days	126	63.0	100.0
Total	200	100.0	

Source: primary data

Table-4.5 refers to the distribution of the beneficiaries of the MGNREGS by the time lag to get the job. It is observed that 37 percent of the sample beneficiary respondents have got a job with the 15 days of application for the job and 63 percent have got the job in the range of above 15 days from the date of application.

Table-4.6: Time lag to get the wage

Time lag to get the wage	Frequency	Percent	Cumulative Percent
Up to 15	54	27.0	27.0
15-30	120	60.0	87.0
Above 30	26	13.0	100.0
Total	200	100.0	

Source: primary data

Table-4.6 refers to the distribution of the beneficiaries of the MGNREGS by the time lag to get the wage. It is observed that 27 percent of the sample beneficiary respondents have got wage within the 15 days of work completion and 60 percent have got the wage in the range of 15-30 days and above 30 days in the case of 13 percent of the respondents to get the wages from the date of completion of MGNREGS works from the date of completion.

Table-4.7: Sources of information

Sources of information	Frequency	Percent	Cumulative Percent
Mate	128	64.0	64.0
Gram Sabha	55	27.5	91.5
Neighbors	17	8.5	100.0
Total	200	100.0	

Source: primary data

Table-4.7 refers to the distribution of the beneficiaries of the MGNREGS by the sources of information about the benefits and facilities of MGNREGS. It is observed that 64 percent of the sample beneficiary respondents have got the information about MGNREGS with reference to benefits and facilities through a mate in MGNREGS program and the same is made available to 27.5 percent through Gram Sabha and to 8.5 percent of respondents through neighbors.

Table-4.8: Institution through which wages are provided

Institution through which Wages are provided	Frequency	Percent	Cumulative Percent
Post office	160	80.0	80.0
Bank	40	20.0	100.0
Total	200	100.0	

Source: primary data

Table-4.8 refers to the distribution of the beneficiaries of the MGNREGS by their response about wages are provided through which institution. It is observed that 80 percent of the respondents have got wages through the post office and 20 percent of the respondents got the wages through the bank.

Table-4.9: Whether bank accounts opened

Whether bank accounts opened	Frequency	Percent	Cumulative Percent
Yes	160	80.0	80.0
No	40	20.0	100.0
Total	200	100.0	

Source: primary data

Table-4.9 refers to the distribution of the beneficiaries of the MGNREGS by their response about whether bank accounts are opened or not. It is observed that 80 percent of the respondents have opened the bank accounts and 20 percent of the respondents did not get opened their bank accounts.

Table-4.10: Corruption for getting job cards

Corruption for getting job cards	Frequency	Percent	Cumulative Percent
Yes	52	26.0	26.0
No	148	74.0	100.0
Total	200	100.0	

Source: primary data

Table-4.10 refers to the distribution of the beneficiaries of the MGNREGS by their response about whether any kind of corruption involved in getting job cards. It is observed that 26 percent of the respondents have opined that there is some amount of corruption involved in getting the job cards and the majority of the respondents (74 %) did not subscribe to the view that there is corruption practice involved in getting the job cards.

Table-4.11: The approach of employees towards MGNREGS

The approach of employees towards MGNREGS	Frequency	Percent	Cumulative Percent
Professional	44	22.0	22.0
Bureaucratic	156	78.0	100.0
Total	200	100.0	

Source: primary data

Table-4.11 refers to the distribution of the beneficiaries of the MGNREGS by their response about the approach of employees towards MGNREGS. It is observed that 44 percent of the respondents have opined that the approach of employees towards MGNREGS is professional and 78 percent of the respondents have felt that the approach of the employees towards the MGNREGS is bureaucratic in nature.

Table-4.12: Politicization of MGNREGS works

Politicization of MGNREGS works	Frequency	Percent	Cumulative Percent
Yes	156	78.0	78.0
No	44	22.0	100.0
Total	200	100.0	

Source: primary data

Table-4.12 refers to the distribution of the beneficiaries of the MGNREGS by their response about the politicization of MGNREGS works. It is observed that 78 percent of the respondents have opined that the works of MGNREGS are politicized and 22 percent of the respondents did not subscribe to this view.

Table-4.13: Communalization of MGNREGS works

Communalization of MGNREGS works	Frequency	Percent	Cumulative Percent
Yes	52	26.0	26.0
No	148	74.0	100.0
Total	200	100.0	

Source: primary data

Table-4.13 refers to the distribution of the beneficiaries of the MGNREGS by their response about communalization of MGNREGS works. It is observed that 26 percent of the respondents have opined that the works of MGNREGS are communalized and 74 percent of the respondents did not subscribe to this view.

Table-4.14: The effectiveness of inspection of MGNREGS Works

The effectiveness of inspection of MGNREGS Works	Frequency	Percent	Cumulative Percent
Low	128	64.0	64.0
Moderate	46	23.0	87.0
High	26	13.0	100.0
Total	200	100.0	

Source: primary data

Table-4.14 refers to the distribution of the beneficiaries of the MGNREGS by their response about the effectiveness of inspection of MGNREGS works. It is observed that the effectiveness of inspection of works of MGNREGS is found to be low for 64 percent and the same is moderate for 23 percent and high in the case of 13 percent of the respondents.

Table-4.15: Awareness levels about 100 day's employment

Awareness levels about 100 day's employment	Frequency	Percent	Cumulative Percent
Low	51	25.5	25.5
Moderate	122	61.0	86.5
High	27	13.5	100.0
Total	200	100.0	

Source: primary data

Table-4.15 refers to the distribution of the beneficiaries of the MGNREGS by their awareness levels about 100 days of employment through MGNREGS works. It is observed that the awareness levels the beneficiaries of MGNREGS about 100 days of employment is found to be low for 25.5 percent of the beneficiaries and the same are moderate for 61 percent and high in the case of 13.5 percent of the respondents.

Table-4.16: Awareness levels about minimum wages

Awareness levels about minimum wages	Frequency	Percent	Cumulative Percent
Low	45	22.5	22.5
Moderate	135	67.5	90.0
High	20	10.0	100.0
Total	200	100.0	

Source: primary data

Table-4.16 refers to the distribution of the beneficiaries of the MGNREGS by their awareness levels about minimum wages through MGNREGS works. It is observed that the awareness levels the beneficiaries of MGNREGS about minimum wages is found to be low for 22.5 percent of the beneficiaries and the same are moderate for 67.5 percent and high in the case of 10 percent of the respondents.

Table-4.17: Awareness levels about equal wages

Awareness levels about equal wages	Frequency	Percent	Cumulative Percent
Low	35	17.5	17.5
Moderate	150	75.0	92.5
High	15	7.5	100.0
Total	200	100.0	

Source: primary data

Table-4.17 refers to the distribution of the beneficiaries of the MGNREGS by their awareness levels about equal wages through MGNREGS works. It is observed that the awareness levels the beneficiaries of MGNREGS about equal wages is found to be low for 17.5 percent of the beneficiaries and the same are moderate for 75 percent and high in the case of 7.5 percent of the respondents.

Table-4.18: Awareness levels about payment mode

Awareness levels about payment mode	Frequency	Percent	Cumulative Percent
Low	54	27.0	27.0
Moderate	117	58.5	85.5
High	29	14.5	100.0
Total	200	100.0	

Source: primary data

Table-4.18 refers to the distribution of the beneficiaries of the MGNREGS by their awareness levels about payment mode of wages through MGNREGS works. It is observed that the awareness levels the beneficiaries of MGNREGS about payment mode of wages through MGNREGS is found to be low for 27 percent of the beneficiaries and the same are moderate for 58.5 percent and high in the case of 14.5 percent of the respondents.

Table-4.19: Awareness levels about stipulated % of women

Awareness levels about stipulated % of women	Frequency	Percent	Cumulative Percent
Low	76	38.0	38.0
Moderate	98	49.0	87.0
High	26	13.0	100.0
Total	200	100.0	

Source: primary data

Table-4.19 refers to the distribution of the beneficiaries of the MGNREGS by their awareness levels about stipulated percent of women in MGNREGS works. It is observed that the awareness levels the beneficiaries of MGNREGS about the stipulated percentage of women in MGNREGS is found to be low for 38 percent of the beneficiaries and the same is moderate for 49 percent and high in the case of 13 percent of the respondents.

Table-4.20: Awareness levels about treatment allowance

Awareness levels about treatment allowance	Frequency	Percent	Cumulative Percent
Low	44	22.0	22.0
Moderate	139	69.5	91.5
High	17	8.5	100.0
Total	200	100.0	

Source: primary data

Table-4.20 refers to the distribution of the beneficiaries of the MGNREGS by their awareness levels about treatment allowance in MGNREGS works. It is observed that the awareness levels the beneficiaries of MGNREGS about treatment allowance in MGNREGS is found to be low for 22 percent of the beneficiaries and the same are moderate for 69.5 percent and high in the case of 8.5 percent of the respondents.

Table-4.21: Awareness levels about crèche

Awareness levels about crèche	Frequency	Percent	Cumulative Percent
Low	62	31.0	31.0
Moderate	118	59.0	90.0
High	20	10.0	100.0
Total	200	100.0	

Source: primary data

Table-4.21 refers to the distribution of the beneficiaries of the MGNREGS by their awareness levels about crèche in MGNREGS works. It is observed that the awareness levels the beneficiaries of MGNREGS about crèche in MGNREGS is found to be low for 31 percent of the beneficiaries and the same are moderate for 59 percent and high in the case of 10 percent of the respondents.

Table-4.22: Awareness levels about the tent for children

Awareness levels about the tent for children	Frequency	Percent	Cumulative Percent
Low	48	24.0	24.0
Moderate	136	68.0	92.0
High	16	8.0	100.0
Total	200	100.0	

Source: primary data

Table-4.22 refers to the distribution of the beneficiaries of the MGNREGS by their awareness levels about the tent for children. It is observed that the awareness levels the beneficiaries of MGNREGS about the tent for children of the MGNREGS workers are found to be low for 24 percent of the beneficiaries and the same are moderate for 68 percent and high in the case of 8 percent of the respondents.

Table-4.23: Awareness levels about water

Awareness levels about water	Frequency	Percent	Cumulative Percent
Low	54	27.0	27.0
Moderate	124	62.0	89.0
High	22	11.0	100.0
Total	200	100.0	

Source: primary data

Table-4.23 refers to the distribution of the beneficiaries of the MGNREGS by their awareness levels about drinking water availability. It is observed that the awareness levels the beneficiaries of MGNREGS about drinking water availability for MGNREGS workers are found to be low for 27 percent of the beneficiaries and the same are moderate for 62 percent and high in the case of 11 percent of the respondents.

Table-4.24: Awareness levels about first aid

Awareness levels about first aid	Frequency	Percent	Cumulative Percent
Low	66	33.0	33.0
Moderate	119	59.5	92.5
High	15	7.5	100.0
Total	200	100.0	

Source: primary data

Table-4.24 refers to the distribution of the beneficiaries of the MGNREGS by their awareness levels about first aid availability. It is observed that the awareness levels the beneficiaries of MGNREGS about first aid availability for MGNREGS workers is found to be low for 33 percent of the beneficiaries and the same is moderate for 59.5 percent and high in the case of 7.5 percent of the respondents.

Table-4.25: Awareness levels about job card application

Awareness levels about job card application	Frequency	Percent	Cumulative Percent
Low	50	25.0	25.0
Moderate	132	66.0	91.0
High	18	9.0	100.0
Total	200	100.0	

Source: primary data

Table-4.25 refers to the distribution of the beneficiaries of the MGNREGS by their awareness levels about the application for job cards. It is observed that the awareness levels the beneficiaries of MGNREGS about the application of job cards for MGNREGS works is found to be low for 25 percent of the beneficiaries and the same are moderate for 66 percent and high in the case of 9 percent of the respondents.

Table-4.26: Awareness levels about women inclusion policy of 33%

Awareness levels about women inclusion policy of 33%	Frequency	Percent	Cumulative Percent
Low	72	36.0	36.0
Moderate	116	58.0	94.0
High	12	6.0	100.0
Total	200	100.0	

Source: primary data

Table-4.26 refers to the distribution of the beneficiaries of the MGNREGS by their awareness levels about women inclusion policy of 3 percent. It is observed that the awareness levels the beneficiaries of MGNREGS about women inclusion policy of 3 percent in MGNREGS works is found to be low for 36 percent of the beneficiaries and the same are moderate for 58 percent and high in the case of 6 percent of the respondents.

Table-4.27: Impact of MGNREGS on household's expenditure

Impact of MGNREGS on household's expenditure	Frequency	Percent	Cumulative Percent
Increased	134	67.0	67.0
Decreased	25	12.5	79.5
Constant	41	20.5	100.0
Total	200	100.0	

Source: primary data

Table-4.27 refers to the distribution of the beneficiaries of the MGNREGS by their about the impact of MGNREGS on household expenditure. It is observed that the 67 percent of the beneficiaries of the MGNREGS has stated that their household expenditure has increased due to the additional income that they got from MGNREGS works and the same has decreased in case of 12.5 percent of the respondents and remained constant in the case of 20.5 percent of the respondents.

Table-4.28: Impact of MGNREGS on migration

Impact of MGNREGS on migration	Frequency	Percent	Cumulative Percent
Increased	34	17.0	17.0
Decreased	59	29.5	46.5
Constant	107	53.5	100.0
Total	200	100.0	

Source: primary data

Table-4.28 refers to the distribution of the beneficiaries of the MGNREGS by their about the impact of MGNREGS on migration. It is observed that the 17 percent of the beneficiaries of the MGNREGS has stated that their migration has increased despite MGNREGS works and the same has decreased in case of 29.5 percent of the respondents and remained constant in the case of 53.5 percent of the respondents.

Table-4.29: Impact of MGNREGS on economic conditions

Impact of MGNREGS on economic conditions	Frequency	Percent	Cumulative Percent
Increased	162	81.0	81.0
Decreased	10	5.0	86.0
Constant	28	14.0	100.0
Total	200	100.0	

Source: primary data

Table-4.29 refers to the distribution of the beneficiaries of the MGNREGS by their about the impact of MGNREGS on economic conditions. It is observed that the 81 percent of the beneficiaries of the MGNREGS have stated that their economic conditions have improved due to MGNREGS works and the same have declined in case of 5 percent of the respondents and remained constant in the case of 14 percent of the respondents.

Table-4.30: Impact of MGNREGS on children education

Impact of MGNREGS on children education	Frequency	Percent	Cumulative Percent
Positive	150	75.0	75.0
Negative	12	6.0	81.0
Statues quo	38	19.0	100.0
Total	200	100.0	

Source: primary data

Table-4.30 refers to the distribution of the beneficiaries of the MGNREGS by their about the impact of MGNREGS on children education. It is observed that the 75 percent of the beneficiaries of the MGNREGS have stated that there is a positive impact of MGNREGS on children education and the said impact is negative for 6 percent of the respondents and remained constant in the case of 19 percent of the respondents.

Table-4.31: Impact of MGNREGS on changes in cultural life

Impact of MGNREGS on changes in cultural life	Frequency	Percent	Cumulative Percent
Positive	124	62.0	62.0
Negative	52	26.0	88.0
Statues quo	24	12.0	100.0
Total	200	100.0	

Source: primary data

Table-4.31 refers to the distribution of the beneficiaries of the MGNREGS by their about the impact of MGNREGS on changes in cultural life. It is observed that the 75 percent of the beneficiaries of the MGNREGS have stated that there is a positive impact of MGNREGS on changes in their cultural life and the said impact is negative for 26 percent of the respondents and remained constant in the case of 12 percent of the respondents.

Table-4.32: Impact of MGNREGS on absolute poverty

Impact of MGNREGS on absolute poverty	Frequency	Percent	Cumulative Percent
Increased	12	6.0	6.0
Decreased	156	78.0	84.0
Constant	32	16.0	100.0
Total	200	100.0	

Source: primary data

Table-4.32 refers to the distribution of the beneficiaries of the MGNREGS by their about the impact of MGNREGS on absolute poverty. It is observed that the 6 percent of the beneficiaries of the MGNREGS have stated that their absolute poverty has increased despite MGNREGS works and the absolute poverty of 78 percent of the beneficiaries has declined which can be attributable to MGNREGS works and for 16 percent of the respondents, their absolute poverty level has remained constant.

Table-4.33: Impact of MGNREGS on unemployment

Impact of MGNREGS on Unemployment	Frequency	Percent	Cumulative Percent
Increased	18	9.0	9.0
Decreased	146	73.0	82.0
Constant	36	18.0	100.0
Total	200	100.0	

Source: primary data

Table-4.33 refers to the distribution of the beneficiaries of the MGNREGS by their about the impact of MGNREGS on unemployment. It is observed that the 9 percent of the beneficiaries of the MGNREGS have stated that their unemployment increased despite MGNREGS works and unemployment of 73 percent of the beneficiaries has declined which can be attributable to MGNREGS works and for 18 percent of the respondents, their unemployment level has remained constant

Table-4.34: Whether the RTI act is effectively used

Whether the RTI act is effectively used	Frequency	Percent	Cumulative Percent
Yes	58	29.0	29.0
No	142	71.0	100.0
Total	200	100.0	

Source: primary data

Table-4.34 refers to the distribution of the beneficiaries of the MGNREGS by their response about a question of whether RTI act is effectively used in the case of MGNREGS. It is observed that 29 percent of the respondents have stated that they have effectively used the RTI act in the case of MGNREGS and 71 percent of the respondents did not subscribe to this view.

Table-4.35: Performance of MGNREGS in sample areas

S. No	Indicators	Palavaram	Peddara-vulapally	Gooda-poor	Mallapr-ajpally	Chiruma-rthy
1	Number of households with Job cards	26700	31152	28650	25395	26544
2	Number of households demanded works	29950	36415	31550	28355	29500
3	Number of employment days generated (in lakhs)	2002500	2149488	1919550	2006205	1698816
4	Average number of days of employment per household	75	69	67	79	64
5	Share of women employment (%)	58.10	35.25	87.29	39.42	55.06
6	Share of SC&ST in employment (%)	39.38	47.47	22.10	51.24	37.12

Source: primary data

Table: 4.35 Shows the distribution of an average number of days of employment by study area. It is observed that Mallaprajpally stands first in terms of an average number of days of employment per households and Chirumarthy stands the last in terms of the said variable. With reference to percent of women employment, Goodapoor stands first (87.29%) and Peddaravulapally stands in the last position. With reference to the share of SC&ST in employment percent, Mallaprajpally stands first (51.24%) and Chirumarthy stands the last.

Table-4.36: Age distribution of sample respondents

S. No	Caste	Palava-ram	Peddara-vulapally	Gooda-poor	Mallapr-ajpally	Chiruma-rthy	Total
1	25 and Below	6	3	12	3	5	29
2	26-35	10	7	5	8	7	37
3	36-45	8	12	7	12	8	47
4	46-55	10	8	8	13	14	53
5	56-65	4	9	8	4	5	30
6	Above 65	2	1	-	-	1	4
	Total	40	40	40	40	40	200

Source: primary data

Table-4.36 analyzes the distribution of the sample respondents by their age in the study area. It is observed that 50 percent of the sample respondents are from the age range of 36-55 years and only 17 percent of the respondents are from above 55 years age range. Thus, the majority of the beneficiaries of MGNREGS are relatively young.

Table-4.37: Caste wise distribution of sample respondents

S. No	Caste	Palava-ram	Peddara-vulapally	Gooda-poor	Mallapr-ajpally	Chiruma-rthy	Total
1	SC	21	19	23	23	22	108
2	ST	3	2	1	3	2	11
3	OBC	8	9	8	5	5	35
4	Minorities	3	6	4	7	6	26
5	OC	5	4	4	2	5	20
	Total	40	40	40	40	40	200

Source: primary data

Table-4.37 analyzes the distribution of the sample respondents by their caste in the study area. It is observed that 54 percent of the sample respondents are from scheduled castes, followed by

17.5 percent are OBCs and only 10 percent are from socially advanced castes.

Table-4.38: Education wise distribution of sample respondents

S. No	Education	Palava-ram	Peddara-vulapally	Gooda-poor	Mallapr-ajpally	Chiruma-rthy	Total
1	Illiterate	29	30	16	20	22	117
2	Primary	10	5	10	13	9	47
3	Secondary	1	5	13	6	7	32
4	High School and Above	-	-	1	1	2	4
	Total	40	40	40	40	40	200

Source: primary data

Table-4.38 analyzes the distribution of the sample respondents by their education in the study area. It is observed that 58.5 percent of the sample respondents are illiterates, followed by 23.5 from the education range of primary level and 16 percent are from secondary education. Thus, it is observed that the education level is poor in the case of the majority of the respondents.

Table-4.39: Marital status of distribution of sample respondents

S. No	Marital status	Palava-ram	Peddara-vulapally	Gooda-poor	Mallapr-ajpally	Chiruma-rthy	Total
1	Married	30	28	35	28	36	157
2	Unmarried	6	8	3	5	3	25
3	Widow	3	2	1	4	1	11
4	Divorce	-	2	1	2	-	5
5	Deserted	1	-	-	1	-	2
	Total	40	40	40	40	40	200

Source: primary data

Table-4.39 analyzes the distribution of the sample respondents by their marital status in the study area. It is observed that 78.5

percent of the sample respondents are married, followed by 12.5 are unmarried and 5.5 percent are widows.

Table-4.40: Occupation wise distribution of sample respondents

S. No	Occupation	Palava-ram	Peddara-vulapally	Gooda-poor	Mallapr-ajpally	Chiruma-rthy	Total
1	Cultivator	3	2	1	4	2	12
2	Agriculture labour	26	26	29	17	26	124
3	Non-Agri. Labour	8	10	7	16	11	52
4	Artisan	2	1	1	2	-	6
5	Business	-	1	1	1	-	3
6	Services	1	-	1	-	1	3
	Total	40	40	40	40	40	200

Source: primary data

Table-4.40 analyzes the distribution of the sample respondents by their occupation in the study area. It is observed that 62 percent of the sample respondents are agriculture laborers, followed by 26 are non-agriculture laborers and only 6 percent are cultivators. Thus, MGNREGS has benefited mostly agriculture and non-agriculture laborers.

Table-4.41: Number of earning members in the households

Particulars	Palava-ram	Peddara-vulapally	Gooda-poor	Mallapr-ajpally	Chiruma-rthy	Total
Average size of earners/House holds	2.4	3.7	2.1	2.3	2.6	2.62
Economic dependency	1.2	1.4	1.1	1.3	1.2	1.24
Earning females	88.5	79.1	72.4	68.5	76.6	77.02

Source: primary data

Table-4.41 analyzes the distribution of the sample respondents by the earning members in the study area. It is observed that the average size of earners per a household is 2.62 members followed by earning females are 77.02 percent and economic dependency is only 1.24.

Table-4.42: Land holding status of the respondents (%)

S. No	Occupation	Palava-ram	Peddara-vulapally	Gooda-poor	Mallapr-ajpally	Chiruma-rthy	Total
1	Landless	19	19	21	21	29	109
2	1 or Below 1 acre	12	13	15	9	6	55
3	1.01-2.5 acres	3	1	2	4	2	12
4	2.51-5.0 acres	4	6	2	5	2	19
5	5.01-10.0 acres	2	1	-	1	1	5
	Total	40	40	40	40	40	200

Source: primary data

Table-4.42 analyzes the distribution of the sample respondents by the landholding status in the study area. It is observed that 54.5 percent of the respondents are landless followed by 33.5 percent are only marginal farmers. It is further observed that only 9.5 percent of small farmers and 2.5 percent of medium farmers have taken part as laborers under MGNREGS.

Table-4.43: Land ownership status of the respondents

	Response	Palava-ram	Peddara-vulapally	Gooda-poor	Mallapr-ajpally	Chiruma-rthy
Land in respondents name	No	192	142	140	176	180
	Yes	8	58	60	24	20
Total		200	200	200	200	200

Source: primary data

Table-4.43 analyzes the distribution of the sample respondents by the land ownership status in the study area. It is observed that

90 percent of the respondents don't have land in their name and only 10 percent of the respondents have got the land in their name.

Table-4.44: Income earned from MGNREGS by the family (Rs)

S. No	Income range (Rs)	Palava-ram	Peddara-vulapally	Gooda-poor	Mallapr-ajpally	Chiruma-rthy	Total
1	Up to 8000	30	23	27	31	32	143
2	8001-16000	10	15	12	8	7	52
3	16001-24000	-	2	1	1	1	5
	Total	40	40	40	40	40	200
	Average income	9657	5090	6543	8352	7658	

Source: primary data

Table-4.44 analyzes the distribution of the sample respondents by the income earned in the study area. It is observed that 71.5 percent of the respondents have got income in the range of up to 8000 rupees followed by 26 percent respondents got income in the range of 8001-16000 rupees and 2.5 percent got income in the range of 16001-24000 rupees. It is further observed that palavaram stands first in terms of average income from MGNREGS and Peddaravulapally stands in the last with reference to the said variable.

Table-4.45: Status of respondents' membership in village development organizations (Multiple responses)

S. No	Institution/ VDO	Palava-ram	Peddara-vulapally	Gooda-poor	Mallapr-ajpally	Chiruma-rthy	Total
1	SHG	100	100	100	85	83	93.6
2	GP	2	8	12	4	6.8	5.7
3	Watershed	1	2	1	-	1	1.2
4	Others	5	2	4	3	2	3.7

Source: primary data

Table-4.45 analyzes the distribution of the sample respondents by the status of respondents' membership in village development organizations in the study area. It is observed that 93.6 percent of the respondents are involved in Self Help Groups, followed by 5.7 percent in Grampanchayat, 1.2 percent in the watershed and 3.7 percent in others.

Table-4.46: Number of times respondents availed loan (%)

S. No	Number of times availed of loans	Palava-ram	Peddara-vulapally	Gooda-poor	Mallapr-ajpally	Chiruma-rthy	Total
1	Not even once	3.0	51.3	35	81	32	42.1
2	1-2 times	35.0	48.8-	40	12	38	33.2
3	3-4 times	41.0	-	16	6	15	16.6
4	5-6 times	20.0	-	9	1	8	7.9
5	Above 6 times	1.0	-	-	-	7	0.3
	Total	100.0	100.0	100.0	100.0	100.0	100.00

Source: primary data

Table-4.46 analyzes the distribution of the sample respondents by the number of times the respondents' availed loan in the study area. It is observed that 42.1 percent of the respondents did not avail the loan at all. It is further observed that 33.2 percent of the respondents have availed the loan 1-2 times and 16.6 percent of the respondents have availed the loan in 3-4 times so far.

Table-4.47: Social Capital and SHG

S. No	Particulars	Palava-ram	Peddara-vulapally	Gooda-poor	Mallapr-ajpally	Chiruma-rthy	Total
1	SHG meetings	97	98.8	86	79	81	88.36
2	Gram Sabha/VDC meetings	88	80	84	59	63	74.8

S. No	Particulars	Palava-ram	Peddara-vulapally	Gooda-poor	Mallapr-ajpally	Chiruma-rthy	Total
3	Village developmental activities	65	71	59	73	81	69.8
4	CBOs (education, watershed, VSS, tec.)	25	31	27	19	18	24
5	Tackling social issues (alcoholism, dowry, etc)	45	35	72	47	51	50
6	Whether taken up any group IGP	70	73	49	52	68	62.4
7	Helping other members of your group	95	79	81	59	72	77.2
	Score	69.28	66.82	65.42	55.42	62	63.79

Source: primary data

Table-4.47 analyzes the distribution of the sample respondents by the social capital in the study area. It is observed that Palavaram stands first in terms of social capital and Mallaprajpally stands in the last with reference to social capital. Meetings of the SHGs followed by helping other members and taking part in Gramsabha are considered to be important forms of social capital.

Table-4.48: Decision making by women of MGNREGS at the household level (%)

S. No	Items	Palava-ram	Peddara-vulapally	Gooda-poor	Mallapr-ajpally	Chiruma-rthy	Total
1	Food	64	60	71	69	65	65.8
2	Clothing	61	57	63	70	61	62.4
3	Children's education	22	25	27	32	29	27.0

S. No	Items	Palava-ram	Peddara-vulapally	Gooda-poor	Mallapr-ajpally	Chiruma-rthy	Total
4	Children marriage	5	10	12	17	21	13.0
5	Attending social gatherings	3	9	11	10	8	8.2
6	Visiting relatives	3	12	15	18	22	14.0
7	Expenditure on self	28	31	19	26	21	25.0
8	Purchasing of assets	8	15	21	22	25	18.2
	Percent of women's participation in house hold decision	24.25	27.38	29.88	33	31.5	29.2

Source: primary data

Table-4.48 analyzes the distribution of the sample respondents by the decision making by the women in MGNREGP in the study area. It is observed that Mallaprajpally stands first in terms of percentage of women's participation and Peddaravulapally stands in the last with reference to the said variable. Attending social gatherings is an activity identified where women's decision-making ability is low.

Table-4.49: Awareness about rights and entitlements provided in NREGS

S. No	Particulars	Palava-ram	Peddara-vulapally	Gooda-poor	Mallapr-ajpally	Chiruma-rthy	Total
1	Right to work	100	98	96	90	81	93.0
2	Right to information	76	59	63	79	80	71.4
3	Maximum number of days of guaranteed employment (100 days)	100	95	98	99	100	98.4

S. No	Particulars	Palava-ram	Peddara-vulapally	Gooda-poor	Mallapr-ajpally	Chiruma-rthy	Total
4	Unemployment allowance	56	53	45	53	65	54.4
5	Wages to be paid if work is given beyond 5 KMS (10more)	79	81	85	67	82	78.8
6	Minimum wages	100	100	100	100	100	100
7	Time limit for providing employment after submission of application	57	64	59	62	55	59.4
8	Time limit for payment of wages (15days)	61	72	83	57	49	64.4
	Sub total score	78.62	77.8	78.63	75.9	76.5	77.5

Source: primary data

Table-4.49 analyzes the distribution of the sample respondents by their awareness about rights and entitlements in MGNREGS in the study area. It is observed that the awareness is maximum in case of minimum wages and the least awareness is in case of unemployment allowance.

Table-4.50: Awareness about NREGS – sources of information (Agency & Media) (%)

S. No	Particulars	Palava-ram	Peddara-vulapally	Gooda-poor	Mallapr-ajpally	Chiruma-rthy	Total
	A. Agency						
1	GP	35	40	58	85	55	54.6
2	SHG	41	60	53	40	50	48.8
3	Officials	85	80	75	70	65	75.0
4	Rozgar Sevak	57	60	65	53	50	57.0
5	Others	10	5	7	4	3	5.8

S. No	Particulars	Palava-ram	Peddara-vulapally	Gooda-poor	Mallapr-ajpally	Chiruma-rthy	Total
			B. Media				
1	Radio	28	44	25	31	28	31.2
2	Wall writings	15	19	21	25	30	22.0
3	Pamphlets	2	4	6	1	2	3.0
4	Kalajathas	5	1	2	2	2	2.4
5	Films	2	3	1	1	1	1.6
6	News Papers	28	32	27	31	32	30.0
7	Others (meetings)	25	22	20	21	22	22.0

Source: primary data

Table-4.50 analyzes the distribution of the sample respondents by their awareness about sources of information with regard to MGNREGS in the study area. It is observed that awareness is maximum through officials and radio.

Table-4.51: Women's participation in MGNREGS process (%)

S. No	Particulars	Palava-ram	Peddara-vulapally	Gooda-poor	Mallapr-ajpally	Chiruma-rthy	Total
1	Applying for job card	49	52	50	38	46	47.0
2	Applying for work	25	21	32	35	40	30.6
3	Opening bank accounts	61	55	50	35	53	56.8
4	Receiving wages	85	89	73	80	86	82.6
5	Participating in the awareness meetings	25	20	22	21	30	23.6
6	Selection of works in Gram Sabha	11	10	5	14	11	10.2

S. No	Particulars	Palava-ram	Peddara-vulapally	Gooda-poor	Mallapr-ajpally	Chiruma-rthy	Total
7	Participating in the social audit	25	15	20	26	23	21.8
8	Overall	40.14	37.4	36.0	39.8	41.2	38.9

Source: primary data

Table-4.51 analyzes the distribution of the sample respondents by women's participation in the processes of MGNREGP in the study area. It is observed that the women's participation is the highest in the process of receiving wages and minimum in the case of selection of works in Gram Sabha.

Table-4.52: Vulnerability Factors Responsible for Participation in MGNREGS

S. No	Factor	Palava-ram	Peddara-vulapally	Gooda-poor	Mallapr-ajpally	Chiruma-rthy	Total
1	No sufficient agriculture activity	50.0	78.8	48.0	36.0	37.0	49.9
2	Low market wages	41.0	60.0	4.0	18.0	20.0	28.4
3	Migration	27.0	32.5	-	8.0	10.0	15.5
4	Illiteracy	52.0	71.3	15.0	22.0	20.0	36.06
5	Lack of Skills	49.0	61.3	54.0	27.0	25.0	43.26
6	Flood	-	3.8	-	2.0	1.0	1.36
7	Drought	57.0	62.5	-	2.0	3.0	24.9
8	Lack of continuous work	50.0	75.0	37.0	36.0	40.0	47.6
9	Other factors (if any)	10.0	8.6	7.0	11.0	10.0	9.32

Source: primary data

Table- 4.52 analyzes the distribution of the sample respondents by the vulnerability factors which prompted them to go for work in MGNREGS in the study area. It is observed that absence of sufficient agriculture activity and lack of continuous work in alternative forms made them opt for activities of MGNREGS (descending order of endorsement) and the least important factor is identified to be flooded.

Table-4.53: Factors motivating women's participation in MGNREGS (%)

S. No	Factor	Palava-ram	Peddara-vulapally	Gooda-poor	Mallapr-ajpally	Chiruma-rthy	Total
1	Minimum wages	81.0	70.0	51.0	34.0	35.0	54.2
2	Timely wages	81.0	31.2	58.0	15.0	17.0	40.44
3	Work taken up on their own land	78.0	5.0	19.0	8.0	8.0	23.6
4	Beneficial assets	81.0	16.2	45.0	11.0	13.0	33.24
5	Family support	77.0	83.8	71.0	51.0	53.0	67.16
6	More than Market wage	75.0	48.8	15.0	12.0	12.0	32.56
7	Equal wages	75.0	38.8	58.0	69.0	71.0	62.36
8	Group arrangement	80.0	76.2	92.0	13.0	15.0	55.24
9	Mode of payment	80.0	31.2	88.0	29.0	35.0	52.64
10	Work site facilities	81.0	16.2	59.0	16.0	48.0	44.04
11	Attitude of officials	81.0	18.8	48.0	10.0	78.0	47.16
12	Timely employment	81.0	27.5	40.0	9.0	18.0	35.1

S. No	Factor	Palava-ram	Peddara-vulapally	Gooda-poor	Mallapr-ajpally	Chiruma-rthy	Total
13	SHG membership	79.0	86.2	65.0	20.0	25.5	55.14
14	Local NGO encouragement	30.0	47.5	9.0	6.0	7.0	19.9
15	Self esteem	55.0	57.5	80.0	5.0	56.5	40.45

Source: primary data

Table- 4.53 deals with the distribution of the sample respondents by the factors motivating women's participation in MGNREGS in the study area. It is observed that the most important motivating factor for women's participation is family support and the least important factor is local NGO's encouragement.

Table-4.54: Factors hindering women's participation in MGNREGS endorsement by respondents

S. No	Factor	Palava-ram	Peddara-vulapally	Gooda-poor	Mallapr-ajpally	Chiruma-rthy	Total
1	Household work load	46.0	2.5	5.0	1.0	7.5	12.4
2	Own agriculture works	46.0	2.5	5.0	1.0	8.5	12.6
3	Health problems	40.0	33.8	43.0	21.0	38.2	35.2
4	Delayed payment	11.0	88.8	14.0	74.0	44.0	46.36
5	Untimely employment	27.0	82.5	16.0	69.0	30.5	45.0
6	Lower than market wages	19.0	28.8	54.0	24.0	20.0	29.16
7	Unequal wages	4.0	8.8	8.0	8.0	7.8	7.32
8	Group arrangement	16.0	35.0	2.0	6.0	11.5	14.1

S. No	Factor	Palava-ram	Peddara-vulapally	Gooda-poor	Mallapr-ajpally	Chiruma-rthy	Total
9	Gender and caste discrimination	4.0	10.0	-	9.0	1.0	4.8
10	Harassment at worksite	4.0	23.8	1.0	8.0	7.2	8.8
11	Attitude of officials	2.0	47.5	1.0	19.0	18.0	17.5
12	Problems in getting employment	15.0	75.0	15.0	47.0	39.5	38.3
13	Rigid timings	44.0	53.8	27.0	14.0	22.5	32.26
	Other factors (if any)	-	10.1	7.0	-	1.0	3.62

Source: primary data

Table- 4.54 deals with the distribution of the sample respondents by the factors hindering women's participation in MGNREGS in the study area. It is observed that the most important hindering factor for women's participation is delayed wage payments and the least important factor is other factors.

Table-4.55: Quality of life

Quality of life	Factor	Palava-ram	Peddara-vulapally	Gooda-poor	Mallapr-ajpally	Chiruma-rthy	Total
Income levels	No change	-	22.5	8.0	2.9	6.5	7.98
	Change to some extent	74.0	76.2	71.0	70.0	65.5	71.34
	Change to large extent	26.0	1.2	21.0	1.0	5.5	10.94
Food	No change	1.0	26.2	28.0	50.0	15.5	24.14
	Change to some extent	85.0	73.8	55.0	49.0	55.5	63.66
	Change to large extent	14.0	-	17.0	1.0	5.1	7.42

Quality of life	Factor	Palava-ram	Peddara-vulapally	Gooda-poor	Mallapr-ajpally	Chiruma-rthy	Total
Clothing	No change	3.0	52.5	34.0	54.0	46.5	38.0
	Change to some extent	78.0	46.2	52.0	45.0	45.5	53.34
	Change to large extent	19.0	1.2	14.0	1.0	2.0	7.44
Health	No change	3.0	47.5	43.0	82.0	78.0	50.7
	Change to some extent	88.0	48.8	46.0	16.0	28.5	45.46
	Change to large extent	9.0	3.8	11.0	2.0	1.5	5.46
Education	No change	2.0	50.0	47.0	81.0	12.0	38.4
	Change to some extent	87.0	46.2	41.0	18.0	85.0	55.44
	Change to large extent	11.0	3.8	12.0	1.0	3.5	6.26
Housing	No change	1.0	72.5	61.0	94.0	79.5	61.6
	Change to some extent	89.0	25.0	26.0	5.0	26.0	34.2
	Change to large extent	10.0	2.5	13.0	1.0	2.0	5.7

Source: primary data

Table-4.55 deals with the distribution of the sample respondents by the quality of life of worker beneficiaries in MGNREGS in the study area. It is observed that the most important positive effects of MGNREGS with reference to quality parameters are identified to be changed in income and housing.

Table-4.56: Governance practices in MGNREGS- Efficiency

Efficiency	Frequency	Percent	Cumulative Percent
Low	54	27.0	27.0
Moderate	118	59.0	86.0
High	28	14.0	100.0
Total	200	100.0	

Source: primary data

Table-4.56 refers to the distribution of the beneficiaries of the MGNREGS by their response about governance practices in MGNREGS with reference to efficiency. It is observed that governance practices in MGNREGS with reference to efficiency is found to be low for 27 percent of the respondent beneficiaries and the same is moderate for 59 percent and high for 14 percent of the respondents of the study.

Table-4.57: Governance practices in MGNREGS-Effectiveness

Effectiveness	Frequency	Percent	Cumulative Percent
Low	30	15.0	15.0
Moderate	58	29.0	44.0
High	112	56.0	100.0
Total	200	100.0	

Source: primary data

Table-4.57 refers to the distribution of the beneficiaries of the MGNREGS by their response about governance practices in MGNREGS with reference to effectiveness. It is observed that governance practices in MGNREGS with reference to effectiveness are found to be low for 15 percent of the respondent beneficiaries and the same is moderate for 29 percent and high for 56 percent of the respondents.

Table-4.58: Governance practices in MGNREGS-Transparency

Transparency	Frequency	Percent	Cumulative Percent
Low	48	24.0	24.0
Moderate	126	63.0	87.0
High	26	13.0	100.0
Total	200	100.0	

Source: primary data

Table-4.58 refers to the distribution of the beneficiaries of the MGNREGS by their response about governance practices in MGNREGS with reference to transparency. It is observed that governance practices in MGNREGS with reference to transparency are found to be low for 24 percent of the respondent beneficiaries and the same is moderate for 63 percent and high for 13 percent of the respondents.

Table-4.59: Governance practices in MGNREGS-Responsiveness

Responsiveness	Frequency	Percent	Cumulative Percent
Low	120	60.0	60.0
Moderate	52	26.0	86.0
High	28	14.0	100.0
Total	200	100.0	

Source: primary data

Table-4.59 refers to the distribution of the beneficiaries of the MGNREGS by their response about governance practices in MGNREGS with reference to responsiveness. It is observed that governance practices in MGNREGS with reference to responsiveness is found to be low for 60 percent of the respondent beneficiaries and the same is moderate for 26 percent and high for 14 percent of the respondents.

Table-4.60: Governance practices in MGNREGS-inclusiveness

inclusiveness	Frequency	Percent	Cumulative Percent
Low	135	67.5	67.5
Moderate	46	23.0	90.5
High	19	9.5	100.0
Total	200	100.0	

Source: primary data

Table-4.60 refers to the distribution of the beneficiaries of the MGNREGS by their response about governance practices in MGNREGS with reference to inclusiveness. It is observed that governance practices in MGNREGS with reference to inclusiveness is found to be low for 67.5 percent of the respondent beneficiaries and the same is moderate for 23 percent and high for 9.5 percent of the respondents.

Table-4.61: Governance practices in MGNREGS-Accountability

Accountability	Frequency	Percent	Cumulative Percent
Low	20	10.0	10.0
Moderate	132	66.0	76.0
High	48	24.0	100.0
Total	200	100.0	

Source: primary data

Table-4.61 refers to the distribution of the beneficiaries of the MGNREGS by their response about governance practices in MGNREGS with reference to accountability. It is observed that governance practices in MGNREGS with reference to accountability is found to be low for 10 percent of the respondent beneficiaries and the same is moderate for 66 percent and high for 24 percent of the respondents.

Table-4.62: Governance practices in MGNREGS-Consensus based decisions

Consensus based decisions	Frequency	Percent	Cumulative Percent
Low	120	60.0	60.0
Moderate	66	33.0	93.0
High	14	7.0	100.0
Total	200	100.0	

Source: primary data

Table-4.62 refers to the distribution of the beneficiaries of the MGNREGS by their response about governance practices in MGNREGS with reference to consensus-based decisions. It is observed that governance practices in MGNREGS with reference to consensus-based decisions is found to be low for 60 percent of the respondent beneficiaries and the same is moderate for 33 percent and high for 7 percent of the respondents.

Table-4.63: Governance practices in MGNREGS-Rule of law

Rule of law	Frequency	Percent	Cumulative Percent
Low	28	14.0	14.0
Moderate	50	25.0	39.0
High	122	61.0	100.0
Total	200	100.0	

Source: primary data

Table-4.63 refers to the distribution of the beneficiaries of the MGNREGS by their response about governance practices in MGNREGS with reference to rule of law. It is observed that governance practices in MGNREGS with reference to rule of law is found to be low for 14 percent of the respondent beneficiaries and the same is moderate for 25 percent and high for 61 percent of the respondents.

Table-4.64: Governance practices in MGNREGS-Participation

Participation	Frequency	Percent	Cumulative Percent
Low	26	13.0	13.0
Moderate	54	27.0	40.0
High	120	60.0	100.0
Total	200	100.0	

Source: primary data

Table-4.64 refers to the distribution of the beneficiaries of the MGNREGS by their response about governance practices in MGNREGS with reference to participation. It is observed that governance practices in MGNREGS with reference to participation is found to be low for 13 percent of the respondent beneficiaries and the same is moderate for 27 percent and high for 60 percent of the respondents.

Table-4.65: Governance practices in MGNREGS-Overall impact

Over all impact	Frequency	Percent	Cumulative Percent
Low	21	10.5	10.5
Moderate	40	20.0	30.5
High	139	69.5	100.0
Total	200	100.0	

Source: primary data

Table-4.65 refers to the distribution of the beneficiaries of the MGNREGS by their response about the overall impact of governance practices in MGNREGS. It is observed that the overall impact of governance practices on the performance of MGNREGS is found to be low for 10.5 percent of the respondent beneficiaries and the same is moderate for 20 percent and high for 69.5 percent of the respondents.

Table-4.66: Political processes of MGNREGS -Frequency of Gram Sabha

Frequency of Gram Sabha	Frequency	Percent	Cumulative Percent
Once in a year	146	73.0	73.0
Twice in a year	54	27.0	100.0
Total	200	100.0	

Source: primary data

Table-4.66 refers to the distribution of the beneficiaries of the MGNREGS by their response about the political processes of MGNREGS with reference to frequency of Gram Sabha. It is observed that the 73 percent of the sample beneficiaries of MGNREGS have stated that Gram Sabha is conducted once in a year and 27 percent of the respondents have stated that gram sabha is conducted twice in a year.

Table-4.67: Political processes of MGNREGS -Participation in Gram Sabha

Participation in Gram Sabha	Frequency	Percent	Cumulative Percent
Low	132	66.0	66.0
Moderate	46	23.0	89.0
High	22	11.0	100.0
Total	200	100.0	

Source: primary data

Table-4.67 refers to the distribution of the beneficiaries of the MGNREGS by their response about the political processes of MGNREGS with reference to participation in Gram Sabha. It is observed that the 66 percent of the sample beneficiaries of MGNREGS have stated that the participation level in Gram Sabha is low and the same is moderate for in case of 23 percent of the respondents and high in the case of 11 percent of the respondents.

Table-4.68: Political processes of MGNREGS -Decision making at Gram Sabha

Decision making at Gram Sabha	Frequency	Percent	Cumulative Percent
Unilateral	156	78.0	78.0
Multilateral	44	22.0	100.0
Total	200	100.0	

Source: primary data

Table-4.68 refers to the distribution of the beneficiaries of the MGNREGS by their response about the political processes of MGNREGS with reference to decision making in Gram Sabha. It is observed that the 78 percent of the sample beneficiaries of MGNREGS have stated that the decision making at Gram Sabha is unilateral and 22 percent of the respondents have stated that decision making in Gram Sabha is multilateral.

Table-4.69: Political processes of MGNREGS -Management of differences among the stakeholders in Gram Sabha

Management of differences among the stakeholders in Gram Sabha	Frequency	Percent	Cumulative Percent
Individualistic	150	75.0	75.0
Systems approach	50	25.0	100.0
Total	200	100.0	

Source: primary data

Table-4.69 refers to the distribution of the beneficiaries of the MGNREGS by their response about the political processes of MGNREGS with reference to the management of differences among the stakeholders in Gram Sabha. It is observed that the 75 percent of the sample beneficiaries of MGNREGS have stated that the management of differences among the stakeholders in Gram Sabha is managed by following individualistic approach and 25 percent of the respondents have stated that by following systems approach differences among the stakeholders are managed.

Table-4.70: Political processes of MGNREGS -Political bias

Political bias	Frequency	Percent	Cumulative Percent
Low	21	10.5	10.5
Moderate	131	65.5	76.0
High	48	24.0	100.0
Total	200	100.0	

Source: primary data

Table-4.70 refers to the distribution of the beneficiaries of the MGNREGS by their response about the political processes of MGNREGS with reference to political bias in Gram Sabha. It is observed that 10.5 percent of the beneficiaries of the MGNREGS have stated the political bias is low and the same is moderate in the case of 65.5 percent of the respondents and high in the case of 24 percent of the sample beneficiaries.

Table-4.71: Political processes of MGNREGS -Social neutrality

Social neutrality	Frequency	Percent	Cumulative Percent
Low	24	12.0	12.0
Moderate	48	24.0	36.0
High	128	64.0	100.0
Total	200	100.0	

Source: primary data

Table-4.71 refers to the distribution of the beneficiaries of the MGNREGS by their response about the political processes of MGNREGS with reference to social neutrality in Gram Sabha. It is observed that 12 percent of the beneficiaries of the MGNREGS have stated the social neutrality is low and the same is moderate in the case of 24 percent of the respondents and high in the case of 64 percent of the sample beneficiaries.

Table-4.72: Political processes of MGNREGS -Involvement of different political parties

	Frequency	Percent	Cumulative Percent
Low	144	72.0	72.0
Moderate	42	21.0	93.0
High	14	7.0	100.0
Total	200	100.0	

Source: primary data

Table-4.72 refers to the distribution of the beneficiaries of the MGNREGS by their response about the political processes of MGNREGS with reference to the involvement of different political parties in Gram Sabha. It is observed that 72 percent of the beneficiaries of the MGNREGS have stated the involvement of different political parties in the Gram Sabha is low and the same is moderate in the case of 21 percent of the respondents and high in the case of 7 percent of the sample beneficiaries.

Table-4.73: Challenges in the implementation of MGNREGS-Delay in releasing the grants

Delay in releasing the grants	Frequency	Percent	Cumulative Percent
Yes	144	72.0	72.0
No	56	28.0	100.0
Total	200	100.0	

Source: primary data

Table-4.73 refers to the distribution of the beneficiaries of the MGNREGS by their response about the challenges in the implementation of MGNREGS with reference to delay in releasing the grants. It is observed that 72 percent of the beneficiaries of the MGNREGS have stated delay in releasing the grants is a challenge confronting the success of MGNREGS and 28 percent of the respondents did not subscribe to this view.

Table-4.74: Challenges in the implementation of MGNREGS-Predominance of political interests over development interests

Predominance of political interests over development interests	Frequency	Percent	Cumulative Percent
Yes	150	75.0	75.0
No	50	25.0	100.0
Total	200	100.0	

Source: primary data

Table-4.74 refers to the distribution of the beneficiaries of the MGNREGS by their response about the challenges in the implementation of MGNREGS with reference to the predominance of political interests over development interests. It is observed that for 75 percent of the beneficiaries of the MGNREGS predominance of political interests over development interests is a challenge confronting the success of the MGNREGS and 25 percent of the respondents did not subscribe to this view.

Table-4.75: Challenges in the implementation of MGNREGS-Ambiguity in the composition of works

Ambiguity in the composition of works	Frequency	Percent	Cumulative Percent
Yes	161	80.5	80.5
No	39	19.5	100.0
Total	200	100.0	

Source: primary data

Table-4.75 refers to the distribution of the beneficiaries of the MGNREGS by their response about the challenges in the implementation of MGNREGS with reference to ambiguity in the composition of works. It is observed that for 80.5 percent of the beneficiaries of the MGNREGS, ambiguity in the composition of MGNREGS works is a challenge confronting the success of the MGNREGS and 19.5 percent of the respondents did not subscribe to this view.

Table-4.76: Challenges in the implementation of MGNREGS-Lack of full support from the beneficiaries

Lack of full support from the beneficiaries	Frequency	Percent	Cumulative Percent
Yes	53	26.5	26.5
No	147	73.5	100.0
Total	200	100.0	

Source: primary data

Table-4.76 refers to the distribution of the beneficiaries of the MGNREGS by their response about the challenges in the implementation of MGNREGS with reference to lack of full support from the beneficiaries. It is observed that for 26.5 percent of the beneficiaries of the MGNREGS, lack of full support from the beneficiaries is a challenge confronting the success of the MGNREGS and 73.5 percent of the respondents did not subscribe to this view.

Table-4.77: Challenges in the implementation of MGNREGS-Low convergence of the related programs

Low convergence of the related programs	Frequency	Percent	Cumulative Percent
Yes	142	71.0	71.0
No	58	29.0	100.0
Total	200	100.0	

Source: primary data

Table-4.77 refers to the distribution of the beneficiaries of the MGNREGS by their response about the challenges in the implementation of MGNREGS with reference to low convergence of the related programs. It is observed that for 71 percent of the beneficiaries of the MGNREGS, low-level convergence of the related programs with MGNREGS works is a challenge confronting the success of the MGNREGS and 29 percent of the respondents did not subscribe to this view.

Table-4.78: Challenges in the implementation of MGNREGS-Failure to forge social capital

Failure to forge social capital	Frequency	Percent	Cumulative Percent
Yes	148	74.0	74.0
No	52	26.0	100.0
Total	200	100.0	

Source: primary data

Table-4.78 refers to the distribution of the beneficiaries of the MGNREGS by their response about the challenges in the implementation of MGNREGS with reference to the failure to forge social capital. It is observed that for 74 percent of the beneficiaries of the MGNREGS, failure to forge social capital in MGNREGS works is a challenge confronting the success of the MGNREGS and 26 percent of the respondents did not subscribe to this view.

Table-4.79: Expectatior -High wage rate

High wage rate	Frequency	Percent	Cumulative Percent
Yes	152	76.0	76.0
No	48	24.0	100.0
Total	200	100.0	

Source: primary data

Table-4.79 refers to the distribution of the beneficiaries of the MGNREGS by their response about their expectations from MGNREGS with reference to high wage rates. It is observed that 76 percent of the beneficiaries of the MGNREGS have expected high wage ra'e from MGNREGS programs and 24 percent of the respondents did not expect the same.

Table-4.80: Expectations-More man-days of employment

More man-days of employment	Frequency	Percent	Cumulative Percent
Yes	136	68.0	68.0
No	64	32.0	100.0
Total	200	100.0	

Source: primary data

Table-4.80 refers to the distribution of the beneficiaries of the MGNREGS by their response about their expectations from MGNREGS with reference to mare man-days of employment. It is observed that 68 percent of the beneficiaries of the MGNREGS have expected more man-days of employment from MGNREGS programs and 32 percent of the respondents did not expect the same.

Table-4.81: Expectations-Measures to promote agri. business

Measures to promote agri. business	Frequency	Percent	Cumulative Percent
Yes	143	71.5	71.5
No	57	28.5	100.0
Total	200	100.0	

Source: primary data

Table-4.81 refers to the distribution of the beneficiaries of the MGNREGS by their response about their expectations from MGNREGS with reference to the promotion of agri. business. It is observed that 71.5 percent of the beneficiaries of the MGNREGS have expected promotion of agribusiness through MGNREGS programs and 28.5 percent of the respondents did not expect the same.

Table-4.82: Expectations-Development of common property resources

Development of common property resources	Frequency	Percent	Cumulative Percent
Yes	141	70.5	70.5
No	59	29.5	100.0
Total	200	100.0	

Source: primary data

Table-4.82 refers to the distribution of the beneficiaries of the MGNREGS by their response about their expectations from MGNREGS with reference to the development of common property resources. It is observed that 70.5 percent of the beneficiaries of the MGNREGS have expected the development of common property resources through MGNREGS programs and 29.5 percent of the respondents did not expect the same.

Table-4.83: Expectations-Community agriculture works

Community agriculture works	Frequency	Percent	Cumulative Percent
Yes	160	80.0	80.0
No	40	20.0	100.0
Total	200	100.0	

Source: primary data

Table-4.83 refers to the distribution of the beneficiaries of the MGNREGS by their response about their expectations from

MGNREGS with reference to community agricultural works. It is observed that 80 percent of the beneficiaries of the MGNREGS have expected the development of community agriculture works through MGNREGS programs and 20 percent of the respondents did not expect the same.

Table-4.84: Expectations-Thorough social audit

Thorough social audit	Frequency	Percent	Cumulative Percent
Yes	162	81.0	81.0
No	38	19.0	100.0
Total	200	100.0	

Source: primary data

Table-4.84 refers to the distribution of the beneficiaries of the MGNREGS by their response about their expectations from MGNREGS with reference to thorough social audit. It is observed that 81 percent of the beneficiaries of the MGNREGS have expected a thorough social audit of MGNREGS programs and 19 percent of the respondents did not expect the same.

It is concluded that average wage rate is in the range of 80-90 rupees, majority of the beneficiaries got job after application of 15-30 days, got the wage rate payment in the range of 15-30 days after completion of the works, attainment of financial inclusion in terms of bank accounts, the approach of the beneficiaries is not professional, works are mostly politicized and effectiveness of inspection of MGNREGS works is insignificant.

Chapter-5

ELITE PERCEPTIONS ABOUT MGNREGS

Chapter-V deals with the perceptions of the elite of the MGNREGS. The elite of the said scheme includes ward members, Sarpanches, MPTCs and ZPTCs who are not the beneficiaries of the MGNREGS but they are facilitators of the performance of the program. The variables examined include

- Age
- Social status
- Educational status
- Income
- Gender
- Political party affiliation
- Position
- Improvement in the livelihood of the people
- Performance in other decent work indicators
- economic security
- Gram Sabha's role in NREGS implementation
- NREGS and corruption
- A role for middlemen in NREGS
- Works taken up in drought-affected areas
- NREGS improved women empowerment
- Social audit is effective

- Works displayed in the notice board
- Percentage of women workers involved in NREGS
- Integration of NREGS with DWACRA
- Water conservation and harvesting
- Flood control and protection
- Micro-irrigation
- Land development of SCs and STs
- Rural connectivity
- Other works
- Transparency in the muster roll
- Selection of NREGS works
- Improvement in community assets

Table-5.1 Position

Position	Frequency	Percent	Cumulative Percent
Ward member	38	76.0	76.0
Sarpanch	5	10.0	86.0
MPTC	5	10.0	96.0
ZPTC	2	4.0	100.0
Total	50	100.0	

Source: Primary Data

Table-5.1 refers to the distribution of the elite respondents by their position. It is found that 76 percent of the elite respondents are ward members, 10 percent are Sarpanches, 10 percent are MPTCs, and ZPTC are 4 percent of the respondents.

Table-5.2 Age of the ward members

Age(in years)	Frequency	Percent	Cumulative Percent
20-35	11	28.9	28.9
35-50	22	57.9	86.8
Above 50	5	13.2	100.0
Total	38	100.0	

Source: primary data

Table-5.2 refers to the distribution of the elite respondents namely ward members by their age. It is found that 28.9 percent of the elite respondents namely ward members are drawn from the age range of 25-35 years, followed by 57.9 percent from 35-50 years age range, and 13.2 percent of the respondents from the age range of above 50 years.

Table-5.3 The social status of the ward members

Social category	Frequency	Percent	Cumulative Percent
OC	8	21.1	21.1
BC	14	36.8	57.9
SC	7	18.4	76.3
ST	5	13.2	89.5
Others	4	10.5	100.0
Total	38	100.0	

Source: primary data

Table-5.3 refers to the distribution of the elite respondents namely ward members by their social status. It is found that 21.1 percent of the elite respondents namely ward members are drawn from the socially advanced castes, 36.8 percent are drawn from backward castes, 18.4 percent are drawn from scheduled castes, 13.2 percent are drawn from scheduled tribes and 10.5 percent are drawn from others.

Table-5.4 Educational status of the ward members

Education level	Frequency	Percent	Cumulative Percent
Literate	12	31.6	31.6
Up to school level	22	57.9	89.5
Above school level	4	10.5	100.0
Total	38	100.0	

Source: primary data

Table-5.4 refers to the distribution of the elite respondents namely ward members by their educational status. It is found that 31.6 percent of the elite respondents namely ward members are equipped with just literacy level, followed by 57.9 percent of the ward members are equipped with up to school level education and 10.5 percent are equipped with above school level education.

Table-5.5 Income of the ward members

Rs.	Frequency	Percent	Cumulative Percent
Up to 60000	22	57.9	57.9
60000-120000	10	26.3	84.2
Above 120000	6	15.8	100.0
Total	38	100.0	

Source: primary data

Table-5.5 refers to the distribution of the elite respondents namely ward members by their income. It is found that 57.9 percent of the elite respondents namely ward members are drawn from the income range of up to 60000 rupees followed by 26.3 percent of the ward members from the income range of 60000-120000 rupees and 15.8 percent are from the income range of above 120000 rupees.

Table-5.6 Gender of the ward members

Gender	Frequency	Percent	Cumulative Percent
Male	24	63.2	63.2
Female	14	36.8	100.0
Total	38	100.0	

Source: primary data

Table-5.6 refers to the distribution of the elite respondents namely ward members by their gender. It is found that 63.2 percent of the elite respondents namely ward members are male and 36.8 percent of the ward members are female.

Table-5.7 Political party affiliation of the ward members

	Frequency	Percent	Cumulative Percent
CPM	3	7.9	7.9
CPI	3	7.9	15.8
Congress	11	28.9	44.7
TDP	12	31.6	76.3
BJP	4	10.5	86.8
TRS	5	13.2	100.0
Total	38	100.0	

Source: primary data

Table-5.7 refers to the distribution of the elite respondents namely ward members by their political party affiliation. It is found that 31.6 percent of the elite respondents namely ward members have got their political affiliation with TDP, followed by 28.9 percent got political affiliation with Congress party, 13.2 percent with TRS, 10.5 percent with BJP,7.9 percent each with CPI and CPM.

Table-5.8 Age of the Sarpanches

Age(in years)	Frequency	Percent	Cumulative ercent
25-35	1	20.0	20.0
35-45	2	40.0	60.0
Above 45	2	40.0	100.0
Total	5	100.0	

Source: primary data

Table-5.8 refers to the distribution of the elite respondents namely Sarpanches by their age. It is found that 20 percent of the elite respondents namely ward members are drawn from the age range of 25-35 years, followed by 40 percent from 35-45 years age range, and 40 percent of the respondents from the age range of above 45 years.

Table-5.9 The social status of the Sarpanches

Social category	Frequency	Percent	Cumulative Percent
OC	1	20.0	20.0
BC	2	40.0	60.0
SC	1	20.0	80.0
ST	1	20.0	100.0
Total	5	100.0	

Source: primary data

Table-5.9 refers to the distribution of the elite respondents namely Sarpanches by their social status. It is found that 20 percent of the elite respondents namely Sarpanches are drawn from the socially advanced castes, 40 percent are drawn from backward castes, 20 percent are drawn from scheduled castes, 20 percent are drawn from scheduled tribes.

Table-5.10 Educational status of the Sarpanches

Education level	Frequency	Percent	Cumulative Percent
Literate	1	20.0	20.0
Up to school level	2	40.0	60.0
Above school level	2	40.0	100.0
Total	5	100.0	

Source: primary data

Table-5.10 refers to the distribution of the elite respondents namely Sarpanches by their educational status. It is found that 20 percent of the elite respondents namely Sarpanches are equipped with just literacy level, followed by 40 percent of the ward members are equipped with up to school level education and 40 percent are equipped with above school level education.

Table-5.11 Income of the Sarpanches

Rs.	Frequency	Percent	Cumulative Percent
Up to100000	1	20.0	20.0
100000-200000	3	60.0	80.0
Above 200000	1	20.0	100.0
Total	5	100.0	

Source: primary data

Table-5.11 refers to the distribution of the elite respondents namely Sarpanches by their income. It is found that 20 percent of the elite respondents namely Sarpanches are drawn from the income range of up to 100000 rupees followed by 60 percent of the Sarpanches from the income range of 100000-200000 rupees and 20 percent are from the income range of above 200000 rupees.

Table-5.12 Gender of the Sarpanches

Gender	Frequency	Percent	Cumulative Percent
Male	3	60.0	60.0
Female	2	40.0	100.0
Total	5	100.0	

Source: primary data

Table-5.12 refers to the distribution of the elite respondents namely Sarpanches by their gender. It is found that 60 percent of the elite respondents namely Sarpanches are male and 40 percent of the Sarpanches are female.

Table-5.13 Political party affiliation of the Sarpanches

	Frequency	Percent	Cumulative Percent
Congress	1	20.0	20.0
CPI	1	20.0	40.0
CPM	1	20.0	60.0
TDP	1	20.0	80.0
TRS	1	20.0	100.0
Total	5	100.0	

Source: primary data

Table-5.13 refers to the distribution of the elite respondents namely Sarpanches by their political party affiliation. It is found that each political party including Congress, CPI, CPM, TDP, TRS has got affiliation from 20 percent of the respondents.

Table-5.14 Age of the MPTC

Age(in years)	Frequency	Percent	Cumulative Percent
35-45	4	80.0	80.0
Above 45	1	20.0	100.0
Total	5	100.0	

Source: primary data

Table-5.14 refers to the distribution of the elite respondents namely MPTCs by their age. It is found that 80 percent of the elite respondents namely MPTC are drawn from the age range of 35-45 years, and 20 percent of the respondents from the age range of above 45 years.

Table-5.15 Social status of the MPTC

Social category	Frequency	Percent	Cumulative Percent
OC	2	40.0	40.0
BC	1	20.0	60.0
SC	1	20.0	80.0
ST	1	20.0	100.0
Total	5	100.0	

Source: primary data

Table-5.15 refers to the distribution of the elite respondents namely MPTCs by their social status. It is found that 40 percent of the elite respondents namely MPTCs are drawn from the socially advanced castes, 20 percent are drawn from backward castes, 20 percent are drawn from scheduled castes, 20 percent are drawn from scheduled tribes.

Table-5.16 Educational status of the MPTC

Education level	Frequency	Percent	Cumulative Percent
Literate	1	20.0	20.0
Up to school level	3	60.0	80.0
Above school level	1	20.0	100.0
Total	5	100.0	

Source: primary data

Table-5.16 refers to the distribution of the elite respondents namely MPTCs by their educational status. It is found that 20 percent of the elite respondents namely MPTCs are equipped with just literacy level, followed by 60 percent of the MPTCs are equipped with up to school level education and 20 percent are equipped with above school level education.

Table-5.17 Income of the MPTC

Rs.	Frequency	Percent	Cumulative Percent
Up to100000	1	20.0	20.0
100000-200000	4	80.0	100.0
Total	5	100.0	

Source: primary data

Table-5.17 refers to the distribution of the elite respondents namely MPTCs by their income. It is found that 20 percent of the elite respondents namely MPTCs are drawn from the income range of up to 100000 rupees and 80 percent of the MPTCs from the income range of 100000-200000 rupees.

Table-5.18 Gender of the MPTC

Gender	Frequency	Percent	Cumulative Percent
Male	2	40.0	40.0
Female	3	60.0	100.0
Total	5	100.0	

Source: primary data

Table-5.18 refers to the distribution of the elite respondents namely MPTCs by their gender. It is found that 40 percent of the elite respondents namely MPTCs are male and 60 percent of the MPTCs are female.

Table-5.19 Political party affiliation of the MPTC

	Frequency	Percent	Cumulative Percent
Congress	1	20.0	20.0
CPI	1	20.0	40.0
CPM	1	20.0	60.0
TDP	1	20.0	80.0
TRS	1	20.0	100.0
Total	5	100.0	

Source: primary data

Table-5.19 refers to the distribution of the elite respondents namely MPTCs by their political party affiliation. It is found that each political party including Congress, CPI, CPM, TDP, and TRS has got affiliation from 20 percent of the respondents.

Table-5.20 Age of the ZPTC

Age(in years)	Frequency	Percent	Cumulative Percent
35-45	1	50.0	50.0
Above 45	1	50.0	100.0
Total	2	100.0	

Source: primary data

Table-5.20 refers to the distribution of the elite respondents namely ZPTCs by their age. It is found that 50 percent of the elite respondents namely ZPTCs are drawn from the age range of 35-45 years, and 50 percent of the respondents from the age range of above 45 years.

Table-5.21 The social status of the ZPTC

Social category	Frequency	Percent	Cumulative Percent
OC	1	50.0	50.0
BC	1	50.0	100.0
Total	2	100.0	

Source: primary data

Table-5.21 refers to the distribution of the elite respondents namely ZPTCs by their social status. It is found that 50 percent of the elite respondents namely ZPTCs are drawn from the socially advanced castes, and 50 percent are drawn from backward castes.

Table-5.22 Educational status of the ZPTC

Education level	Frequency	Percent	Cumulative Percent
Up to school level	1	50.0	50.0
Above school level	1	50.0	100.0
Total	2	100.0	

Source: primary data

Table-5.22 refers to the distribution of the elite respondents namely ZPTCs by their educational status. It is found that 50 percent of the elite respondents namely ZPTCs are equipped with up to school level education and 50 percent are equipped with above school level education.

Table-5.23 Income of the ZPTC

Rs.	Frequency	Percent	Cumulative Percent
100000-200000	2	100.0	100.0

Source: primary data

Table-5.23 refers to the distribution of the elite respondents namely ZPTCs by their income. It is found that 100 percent of the elite respondents namely ZPTCs are drawn from the income range of 100000-200000 rupees.

Table-5.24 Gender of the ZPTC

Gender	Frequency	Percent	Cumulative Percent
Male	1	50.0	50.0
Female	1	50.0	100.0
Total	2	100.0	

Source: primary data

Table-5.24 refers to the distribution of the elite respondents namely ZPTCs by their gender. It is found that 50 percent of the elite respondents namely ZPTCs are male and 50 percent of the ZPTCs are female.

Table-5.25 Political party affiliation of the ZPTC

	Frequency	Percent	Cumulative Percent
Congress	1	50.0	50.0
TDP	1	50.0	100.0
Total	2	100.0	

Source: primary data

Table-5.25 refers to the distribution of the elite respondents namely ZPTCs by their political party affiliation. It is found that 50 percent of ZPTCs are affiliated to Congress and 50 percent are affiliated to TDP.

Table-5.26 Does MGNREGS improve the livelihood of the people?

Does NREGS improve the livelihood of the people	Frequency	Percent	Cumulative Percent
Yes	38	76.0	76.0
No	12	24.0	100.0
Total	50	100.0	

Source: Primary Data

Table-5.26 refers to the distribution of the elite respondents by their response about a question of whether MGNREGS improve the livelihood of the people or not. It is found that 76 percent of the elite respondents are of the opinion that MGNREGS has improved the livelihood of the people which included regular and income with certainty and 24 percent of the respondents did not subscribe to this view.

Table-5.27 Performance in other decent work indicators

Performance in other decent work indicators	Frequency	Percent	Cumulative Percent
Low	12	24.0	24.0
Moderate	31	62.0	86.0
High	7	14.0	100.0
Total	50	100.0	

Source: Primary Data

Table-5.27 refers to the distribution of the elite respondents by their response to the performance in other decent work indicators attributable to MGNREGS. It is observed that the performance in other decent work indicators like fixed hours of work, toilet facilities for women, health insurance etc attributable to MGNREGS is found to be low for 24 percent of the elite respondents, and the same is moderate for 62 percent of the elite respondents and high for 14 percent of the elite respondents.

Table-5.28 Does NREGS provide economic security?

Does NREGS provide economic security	Frequency	Percent	Cumulative Percent
Yes	37	74.0	74.0
No	13	26.0	100.0
Total	50	100.0	

Source: Primary Data

Table-5.28 refers to the distribution of the elite respondents by their response about whether MGNREGS has provided economic security or not. It is observed that 74 percent of the elite respondents have observed that MGNREGS has ensured economic security to them and 26 percent of the respondents did not subscribe to this view.

Table-5.29 Does Gram Sabha play an important role in NREGS implementation

Does Gram Sabha play an important role in NREGS implementation	Frequency	Percent	Cumulative Percent
Yes	22	44.0	44.0
No	28	56.0	100.0
Total	50	100.0	

Source: Primary Data

Table-5.29 refers to the distribution of the elite respondents by their response about whether Gram Sabha played an important role in the implementation of MGNREGS works or not. It is observed that 44 percent of the elite respondents have observed that gramasabha has played an important role in the implementation of the MGNREGS and 56 percent of the respondents did not subscribe to this view.

Table-5.30 Does NREGS is subject to corruption

Does NREGS is subject to corruption	Frequency	Percent	Cumulative Percent
Yes	14	28.0	28.0
No	36	72.0	100.0
Total	50	100.0	

Source: Primary Data

Table-5.30 refers to the distribution of the elite respondents by their response about whether MGNREGS is subject to corruption or not. It is observed that 28 percent of the elite respondents have observed that MGNREGS is subject to corruption and 72 percent of the respondents did not subscribe to this view.

Table-5.31 Is there any role for middlemen in MGNREGS

Is there any role for middlemen in NREGS	Frequency	Percent	Cumulative Percent
Yes	7	14.0	14.0
No	43	86.0	100.0
Total	50	100.0	

Source: Primary Data

Table-5.31 refers to the distribution of the elite respondents by their response about is there any role for middlemen in MGNREGS. It is observed that 14 percent of the elite respondents have observed that some role is there for middlemen in MGNREGS and 86 percent of the respondents did not subscribe to this view.

Table-5.32 Works taken up in drought-affected areas

Works taken up in drought affected areas	Frequency	Percent	Cumulative Percent
Yes	41	82.0	82.0
No	9	18.0	100.0
Total	50	100.0	

Source: Primary Data

Table-5.32 refers to the distribution of the elite respondents by their response about whether works were taken up in drought-affected areas through MGNREGS. It is observed that 82 percent of the elite respondents have observed that works were taken up in drought-affected areas through MGNREGS and 18 percent of the respondents did not subscribe to this view.

Table-5.33 Does NREGS improved women empowerment

Does NREGS improved women empowerment	Frequency	Percent	Cumulative Percent
Yes	42	84.0	84.0
No	8	16.0	100.0
Total	50	100.0	

Source: Primary Data

Table-5.33 refers to the distribution of the elite respondents by their response about whether women empowerment was improved through MGNREGS or not. It is observed that 84 percent of the elite respondents have observed that women empowerment is improved through MGNREGS and 16 percent of the respondents did not subscribe to this view.

Table-5.34 Social audit is effective

Social audit is effective	Frequency	Percent	Cumulative Percent
Yes	32	64.0	64.0
No	18	36.0	100.0
Total	50	100.0	

Source: Primary Data

Table-5.34 refers to the distribution of the elite respondents by their response about whether the social audit is effective or not. It is observed that 64 percent of the elite respondents have stated that social audit in MGNREGS is effective and 36 percent of the respondents did not subscribe to this view.

Table-5.35 Whether works displayed in notice board

Weather works displayed in notice board	Frequency	Percent	Cumulative Percent
Yes	35	70.0	70.0
No	15	30.0	100.0
Total	50	100.0	

Source: Primary Data

Table-5.35 refers to the distribution of the elite respondents by their response about whether MGNREGS works are displayed in the notice board or not. It is observed that 70 percent of the elite respondents have stated that MGNREGS works are displayed in notice board and 30 percent of the respondents did not subscribe to this view.

Table-5.36 Percentage of women workers involved in NREGS

Percentage of women workers involved in NREGS	Frequency	Percent	Cumulative Percent
Up to 26	39	78.0	78.0
26-50	11	22.0	100.0
Total	50	100.0	

Source: Primary Data

Table-5.36 refers to the distribution of the elite respondents by their response about the percentage of women workers involved in MGNREGS. It is observed that 78 percent of the elite respondents have stated that up to 26 percent of women workers are involved in MGNREGS works and 22 percent of the respondents have stated that 26-50 percent of the women workers are involved in MGNREGS works.

Table-5.37 Whether the NREGS is properly integrated with DWACRA

Whether the NREGS is properly integrated with DWACRA	Frequency	Percent	Cumulative Percent
Yes	17	34.0	34.0
No	33	66.0	100.0
Total	50	100.0	

Source: Primary Data

Table-5.37 refers to the distribution of the elite respondents by their response about whether MGNREGS is properly integrated with DWACRA or not. It is observed that 34 percent of the elite respondents have stated that MGNREGS is properly integrated with DWACRA and 66 percent of the respondents did not subscribe to this view.

Table-5.38 Productive asset creation-Water conservation and harvesting

Water conservation and harvesting	Frequency	Percent	Cumulative Percent
Up to 50000	34	68.0	68.0
50000-100000	11	22.0	90.0
Above 100000	5	10.0	100.0
Total	50	100.0	

Source: Primary Data

Table-5.38 refers to the distribution of the elite respondents by their response about the worth of water conservation and harvesting works completed through MGNREGS. It is observed that 68 percent of the elite respondents have stated that through MGNREGS, water conservation and harvesting works worth of up to 50000 rupees is created, and the same is Rs 50000-100000 worth of water conservation and harvesting worth works are created by MGNREGS works as stated by 22 percent and 10 percent of the respondents have stated that the same is above 100000 rupees.

Table-5.39 Productive asset creation-Flood control and protection

Flood control and protection	Frequency	Percent	Cumulative Percent
up to 25000	29	58.0	58.0
25000-50000	14	28.0	86.0
Above 50000	7	14.0	100.0
Total	50	100.0	

Source: Primary Data

Table-5.39 refers to the distribution of the elite respondents by their response about the worth of flood control and protection works completed through MGNREGS. It found that 58 percent of the sample elite respondents have stated that up to 25000 rupees worth flood control and protection assets are created through MGNREGS works and the same is worth of 25000-50000 rupees as endorsed by 28 percent of the respondents and above 50000 rupees as endorsed by 14 percent respondents.

Table-5.40 Productive asset creation-Micro irrigation

Micro irrigation	Frequency	Percent	Cumulative Percent
Up to one lakh	12	24.0	24.0
Above one lakh	38	76.0	100.0
Total	50	100.0	

Source: Primary Data

Table-5.40 refers to the distribution of the elite respondents by their response about the worth of micro irrigation works completed through MGNREGS. It found that 24 percent of the sample elite respondents have stated that up to one lakh rupees worth micro irrigation assets are created through MGNREGS works and the same is worth of above one lakh rupees as endorsed by 76 percent of the respondents.

Table-5.41 Productive asset creation-Land development of SCs and STs

Land development of SCs and STs	Frequency	Percent	Cumulative Percent
Up to 20000	8	16.0	16.0
20000-40000	12	24.0	40.0
Above 40000	30	60.0	100.0
Total	50	100.0	

Source: Primary Data

Table-5.41 refers to the distribution of the elite respondents by their response about the worth of land development of SCs and STs through

MGNREGS. It found that 16 percent of the sample elite respondents have stated that up to 20000 rupees worth of land development works of SCs and STs are completed through MGNREGS, 24 percent of the elite respondents have stated that 20000-40000 rupees worth of land development works of SCs and STs have been completed and the same is worth above 40000 rupees is created through MGNREGS.

Table-5.42 Productive asset creation-Rural connectivity

Rural connectivity	Frequency	Percent	Cumulative Percent
up to 50000	34	68.0	68.0
50000-100000	10	20.0	88.0
Above 100000	6	12.0	100.0
Total	50	100.0	

Source: Primary Data

Table-5.42 refers to the distribution of the elite respondents by their response to the worth of rural connectivity through MGNREGS. It found that through MGNREGS, rural connectivity worth of up to 50000 rupees worth works are created which is endorsed by 68 percent of the elite respondents followed by 50000-100000 rupees worth works created by 20 percent of the respondents and above 100000 worth rural connectivity is created by 12 percent of the respondents. Rural connectivity is improved in terms of roads due to the MGNREGS works undertaken in agricultural areas.

Table-5.43 Productive asset creation-Other works

Other works	Frequency	Percent	Cumulative Percent
up to 10000	32	64.0	64.0
10000-20000	11	22.0	86.0
Above 20000	7	14.0	100.0
Total	50	100.0	

Source: Primary Data

Table-5.43 refers to the distribution of the elite respondents by their response about the worth of other works through MGNREGS.

It found that through MGNREGS, other works worth of up to 10000 rupees worth works are created which is endorsed by 64 percent of the elite respondents followed by 10000-20000 rupees worth work s created by 22 percent of the respondents and above 20000 worth other works is created by 14 percent of the respondents.

Table-5.44 Whether the transparency in muster roll in NREGS is maintained

Whether the transparency in muster roll in NREGS is maintained	Frequency	Percent	Cumulative Percent
Yes	37	74.0	74.0
No	13	26.0	100.0
Total	50	100.0	

Source: Primary Data

Table-5.44 refers to the distribution of the elite respondents by their response about whether transparency in muster roll management is maintained or not. It is found that transparency is maintained in muster roll management which is endorsed by 74 percent of the elite respondents and 26 percent of the respondents did not subscribe to this view.

Table-5.45 NREGS works are selected by

NREGS works are selected by	Frequency	Percent	Cumulative Percent
Gram Sabha	48	96.0	96.0
Officials	2	4.0	100.0
Total	50	100.0	

Source: Primary Data

Table-5.45 refers to the distribution of the elite respondents by their response about who will select MGNREGS works. It is found that 96 percent of the elite respondents have stated that MGNREGS works are selected by Gram Sabha and 4 percent of the elite respondents have stated that the MGNREGS works are selected by officials.

Table-5.46 Improvement in community assets

Improvement in community assets	Frequency	Percent	Cumulative Percent
Improved	33	66.0	66.0
Constant	11	22.0	88.0
Declined	6	12.0	100.0
Total	50	100.0	

Source: Primary Data

Table-5.46 refers to the distribution of the elite respondents by their response about change in the worth of community assets attributable to MGNREGS. It is found that 66 percent of the elite respondents have stated that community assets are improved due to MGNREGS and the same is constant in the case of 22 percent of the elite respondents and declined as endorsed by 12 percent of the elite respondents.

Thus, it is concluded that the majority of the elite have opined that MGNREGS has improved livelihood, ensured economic security, women empowerment is improved, MGNREGS is not properly integrated with DWACRA, infrastructure is improved and community assets are improved.

Chapter-6

CONCLUSIONS

An attempt is made in this chapter to present chapter wise conclusions followed by suggestions.

The study is divided into six chapters. The **chapter-I** covered the significance of the public policy of rural development, MGNREGS and its significance, objectives of the present study, hypotheses, and suitable methodology. It also dealt with a review of the earlier studies, aspects covered, and gaps in those studies.

The **chapter-II** dealt with the review of the literature

The **chapter-III** dealt with the profile of Nalgonda district and with the socio-economic profile of the beneficiaries of MGNREGS which include

- 40 beneficiary respondents covered under MGNREGS palavaram, 40 from Peddaravulapally, 40 from Goodapur, 40 from Mallaprajpally, and 40 from Chirumarthy village are selected.
- 69 percent of the sample beneficiary respondents are male and 31 percent are female.
- 26.5 percent of the sample beneficiary respondents are from the age range of 20-30 years, followed by 58.5 percent from 30-45 years and 15 percent are from above 45 years range. Thus, the majority of the sample beneficiary respondents are found to be relatively young.
- 11 percent of the sample beneficiary respondents are drawn from socially advanced castes, followed by 48 percent are from backward castes, 19 percent are from scheduled castes,

14 percent are from scheduled tribes and 8 percent are from another category. Thus, the majority of the sample beneficiary respondents are drawn from socially downtrodden communities.

- 27 percent of the sample beneficiary respondents are drawn from the joint family system and 73 percent are from nuclear families.
- 29 percent of the sample beneficiary respondents are with agriculture as their occupation and 71 percent of the respondents from caste-based occupations. Thus, the sample composition is predominant with caste-based occupations.
- 28.5 percent of the sample beneficiary respondents are illiterates and 71.5 percent of the respondents are found to be literates.

The **chapter-IV** dealt with the perceptions of the beneficiaries of MGNREGS on its performance which include

- 28.5 percent of the sample beneficiary respondents are illiterates and 71.5 percent of the respondents are found to be literates.
- 29.5 percent of the sample beneficiary respondents have got employment in the range of 40-60 man-days of employment under MGNREGS, and the same is 60-80 man-days of employment for 57.5 percent of the respondents and above 80 days of employment in the case of 13 percent of the respondents.
- 15.5 percent of the sample beneficiary respondents have got wage rate in the range of 70-80 rupees under MGNREGS, and the same is 80-90 rupees for 61 percent of the respondents and above 90 rupees in the case of 23.5 percent of the respondents.
- 37 percent of the sample beneficiary respondents have got the job with the 15 days of application for the job and 63 percent have got the job in the range of above 15 days from the date of application.
- 27 percent of the sample beneficiary respondents have got wage within the 15 days of work completion and 60 percent have got the wage in the range of 15-30 days and above 30 days in the case of 13 percent of the respondents to get the wages from

the date of completion of MGNREGS works from the date of completion.

- 64 percent of the sample beneficiary respondents have got the information about MGNREGS with reference to benefits and facilities through mate in MGNREGS program and the same is made available to 27.5 percent through Gram Sabha and to 8.5 percent of respondents through neighbors.
- 80 percent of the respondents have got wages through the post office and 20 percent of the respondents got the wages through the bank.
- 80 percent of the respondents have opened the bank accounts and 20 percent of the respondents did not get opened their bank accounts.
- 26 percent of the respondents have opined that there is some amount of corruption involved in getting the job cards and the majority of the respondents (74 %) did not subscribe to the view that there is corruption practice involved in getting the job cards.
- 44 percent of the respondents have opined that the approach of employees towards MGNREGS is professional and 78 percent of the respondents have felt that the approach of the employees towards the MGNREGS is bureaucratic in nature.
- 78 percent of the respondents have opined that the works of MGNREGS are politicized and 22 percent of the respondents did not subscribe to this view.
- 26 percent of the respondents have opined that the works of MGNREGS are communalized and 74 percent of the respondents did not subscribe to this view.
- The effectiveness of inspection of works of MGNREGS is found to be low for 64 percent and the same is moderate for 23 percent and high in the case of 13 percent of the respondents.
- The awareness levels the beneficiaries of MGNREGS about 100 days of employment is found to be low for 25.5 percent of

the beneficiaries and the same is moderate for 61 percent and high in the case of 13.5 percent of the respondents.

- The awareness levels the beneficiaries of MGNREGS about minimum wages is found to be low for 22.5 percent of the beneficiaries and the same is moderate for 67.5 percent and high in the case of 10 percent of the respondents.
- The awareness levels the beneficiaries of MGNREGS about equal wages is found to be low for 17.5 percent of the beneficiaries and the same is moderate for 75 percent and high in the case of 7.5 percent of the respondents.
- The awareness levels the beneficiaries of MGNREGS about payment mode of wages through MGNREGS is found to be low for 27 percent of the beneficiaries and the same is moderate for 58.5 percent and high in the case of 14.5 percent of the respondents.
- The awareness levels the beneficiaries of MGNREGS about the stipulated percentage of women in MGNREGS is found to be low for 38 percent of the beneficiaries and the same is moderate for 49 percent and high in the case of 13 percent of the respondents.
- The awareness levels the beneficiaries of MGNREGS about treatment allowance in MGNREGS is found to be low for 22 percent of the beneficiaries and the same is moderate for 69.5 percent and high in the case of 8.5 percent of the respondents.
- The awareness levels the beneficiaries of MGNREGS about crèche in MGNREGS is found to be low for 31 percent of the beneficiaries and the same is moderate for 59 percent and high in the case of 10 percent of the respondents.
- The awareness levels the beneficiaries of MGNREGS about the tent for children of the MGNREGS workers are found to be low for 24 percent of the beneficiaries and the same is moderate for 68 percent and high in the case of 8 percent of the respondents.

- The awareness levels the beneficiaries of MGNREGS about drinking water availability for MGNREGS workers are found to be low for 27 percent of the beneficiaries and the same is moderate for 62 percent and high in the case of 11 percent of the respondents.
- The awareness levels the beneficiaries of MGNREGS about first aid availability for MGNREGS workers are found to be low for 33 percent of the beneficiaries and the same is moderate for 59.5 percent and high in the case of 7.5 percent of the respondents.
- The awareness levels the beneficiaries of MGNREGP about the application of job cards for MGNREGS works is found to be low for 25 percent of the beneficiaries and the same is moderate for 66 percent and high in the case of 9 percent of the respondents.
- The awareness levels the beneficiaries of MGNREGS about women inclusion policy of 33 percent in MGNREGS works is found to be low for 36 percent of the beneficiaries and the same is moderate for 58 percent and high in the case of 6 percent of the respondents.
- 67 percent of the beneficiaries of the MGNREGS have stated that their household expenditure has increased due to the additional income that they got from MGNREGS works and the same has decreased in case of 12.5 percent of the respondents and remained constant in the case of 20.5 percent of the respondents.
- 17 percent of the beneficiaries of the MGNREGS have stated that their migration has increased despite MGNREGS works and the same has decreased in case of 29.5 percent of the respondents and remained constant in the case of 53.5 percent of the respondents.
- 81 percent of the beneficiaries of the MGNREGS have stated that their economic conditions have improved due to MGNREGS works and the same have declined in case of 5 percent of the respondents and remained constant in the case of 14 percent of the respondents.

- The 75 percent of the beneficiaries of the MGNREGS have stated that there is a positive impact of MGNREGS on children education and the said impact is negative for 6 percent of the respondents and remained constant in the case of 19 percent of the respondents.
- The 75 percent of the beneficiaries of the MGNREGS have stated that there is a positive impact of MGNREGS on changes in their cultural life and the said impact is negative for 26 percent of the respondents and remained constant in the case of 12 percent of the respondents.
- 6 percent of the beneficiaries of the MGNREGS have stated that their absolute poverty has increased despite MGNREGS works and the absolute poverty of 78 percent of the beneficiaries has declined which can be attributable to MGNREGS works and for 16 percent of the respondents, their absolute poverty level has remained constant.
- The 9 percent of the beneficiaries of the MGNREGS have stated that their unemployment increased despite MGNREGS works and unemployment of 73 percent of the beneficiaries has declined which can be attributable to MGNREGS works and for 18 percent of the respondents, their unemployment level has remained constant.
- 29 percent of the respondents have stated that they have effectively used the RTI act in the case of MGNREGS and 71 percent of the respondents did not subscribe to this view.
- Governance practices in MGNREGS with reference to efficiency is found to be low for 27 percent of the respondent beneficiaries and the same is moderate for 59 percent and high for 14 percent of the respondents of the study.
- Governance practices in MGNREGS with reference to effectiveness is found to be low for 15 percent of the respondent beneficiaries and the same is moderate for 29 percent and high for 56 percent of the respondents.
- Governance practices in MGNREGS with reference to transparency is found to be low for 24 percent of the respondent

beneficiaries and the same is moderate for 63 percent and high for 13 percent of the respondents.

- Governance practices in MGNREGS with reference to responsiveness is found to be low for 60 percent of the respondent beneficiaries and the same is moderate for 26 percent and high for 14 percent of the respondents.
- Governance practices in MGNREGS with reference to inclusiveness is found to be low for 67.5 percent of the respondent beneficiaries and the same is moderate for 23 percent and high for 9.5 percent of the respondents.
- Governance practices in MGNREGS with reference to accountability is found to be low for 10 percent of the respondent beneficiaries and the same is moderate for 66 percent and high for 24 percent of the respondents.
- Governance practices in MGNREGS with reference to consensus-based decisions is found to be low for 60 percent of the respondent beneficiaries and the same is moderate for 33 percent and high for 7 percent of the respondents.
- Governance practices in MGNREGS with reference to rule of law is found to be low for 14 percent of the respondent beneficiaries and the same is moderate for 25 percent and high for 61 percent of the respondents.
- Governance practices in MGNREGS with reference to participation is found to be low for 13 percent of the respondent beneficiaries and the same is moderate for 27 percent and high for 60 percent of the respondents.
- The overall impact of governance practices on the performance of MGNREGS is found to be low for 10.5 percent of the respondent beneficiaries and the same is moderate for 20 percent and high for 69.5 percent of the respondents.
- The 73 percent of the sample beneficiaries of MGNREGS have stated that Gram Sabha is conducted once in a year and 27 percent of the respondents have stated that gram sabha is conducted twice in a year.

- The 66 percent of the sample beneficiaries of MGNREGS have stated that the participation level in Gram Sabha is low and the same is moderate for in case of 23 percent of the respondents and high in the case of 11 percent of the respondents.
- 78 percent of the sample beneficiaries of MGNREGS have stated that the decision making at Gram Sabha is unilateral and 22 percent of the respondents have stated that decision making in Gram Sabha is multilateral.
- The 75 percent of the sample beneficiaries of MGNREGS have stated that the management of differences among the stakeholders in Gram Sabha is managed by following individualistic approach and 25 percent of the respondents have stated that by following systems approach differences among the stakeholders are managed.
- 10.5 percent of the beneficiaries of the MGNREGS have stated the political bias is low and the same is moderate in the case of 65.5 percent of the respondents and high in the case of 24 percent of the sample beneficiaries.
- 12 percent of the beneficiaries of the MGNREGS have stated the social neutrality is low and the same is moderate in the case of 24 percent of the respondents and high in the case of 64 percent of the sample beneficiaries.
- 72 percent of the beneficiaries of the MGNREGS have stated the involvement of different political parties in the Gram Sabha is low and the same is moderate in the case of 21 percent of the respondents and high in the case of 7 percent of the sample beneficiaries.
- 72 percent of the beneficiaries of the MGNREGS have stated delay in releasing the grants is a challenge confronting the success of MGNREGS and 28 percent of the respondents did not subscribe to this view.
- For 75 percent of the beneficiaries of the MGNREGS predominance of political interests over development, interest is a challenge confronting the success of the MGNREGS and 25 percent of the respondents did not subscribe to this view.

- For 80.5 percent of the beneficiaries of the MGNREGS, ambiguity in the composition of MGNREGS works is a challenge confronting the success of the MGNREGS and 19.5 percent of the respondents did not subscribe to this view.
- For 26.5 percent of the beneficiaries of the MGNREGS, lack of full support from the beneficiaries is a challenge confronting the success of the MGNREGS and 73.5 percent of the respondents did not subscribe to this view.
- For 71 percent of the beneficiaries of the MGNREGS, low-level convergence of the related programs with MGNREGS works is a challenge confronting the success of the MGNREGS and 29 percent of the respondents did not subscribe to this view.
- For 74 percent of the beneficiaries of the MGNREGS, failure to forge social capital in MGNREGS works is a challenge confronting the success of the MGNREGS and 26 percent of the respondents did not subscribe to this view.
- 76 percent of the beneficiaries of the MGNREGS have expected high wage rate from MGNREGS programs and 24 percent of the respondents did not expect the same.
- 68 percent of the beneficiaries of the MGNREGS have expected more man-days of employment from MGNREGS programs and 32 percent of the respondents did not expect the same.
- 71.5 percent of the beneficiaries of the MGNREGS have expected promotion of agribusiness through MGNREGS programs and 28.5 percent of the respondents did not expect the same.
- 70.5 percent of the beneficiaries of the MGNREGS have expected the development of common property resources through MGNREGS programs and 29.5 percent of the respondents did not expect the same.
- 80 percent of the beneficiaries of the MGNREGS have expected the development of community agriculture works through MGNREGS programs and 20 percent of the respondents did not expect the same.

- 81 percent of the beneficiaries of the MGNREGS have expected a thorough social audit of MGNREGS programs and 19 percent of the respondents did not expect the same.

The **Chapter-V** dealt with the perceptions of the elite of MGNREGS on its performance which include

- 76 percent of the elite respondents are ward members, 10 percent are Sarpanches, 10 percent are MPTCs, and ZPTC are 4 percent of the respondents.
- 76 percent of the elite respondents are of the opinion that MGNREGS has improved the livelihood of the people and 24 percent of the respondents did not subscribe to this view.
- The performance in other decent work indicators attributable to MGNREGS is found to be low for 24 percent of the elite respondents, and the same is moderate for 62 percent of the elite respondents and high for 14 percent of the elite respondents.
- 74 percent of the elite respondents have observed that MGNREGS has ensured economic security and 26 percent of the respondents did not subscribe to this view.
- 44 percent of the elite respondents have observed that Gram Sabha has played an important role in the implementation of the MGNREGS and 56 percent of the respondents did not subscribe to this view.
- 28 percent of the elite respondents have observed that MGNREGS is subject to corruption and 72 percent of the respondents did not subscribe to this view.
- 14 percent of the elite respondents have observed that some role is there for middlemen in MGNREGS and 86 percent of the respondents did not subscribe to this view.
- 82 percent of the elite respondents have observed that works were taken up in drought-affected areas through MGNREGS and 18 percent of the respondents did not subscribe to this view.
- 84 percent of the elite respondents have observed that women empowerment is improved through MGNREGS and 16 percent of the respondents did not subscribe to this view. 64 percent of

the elite respondents have stated that social audit in MGNREGS is effective and 36 percent of the respondents did not subscribe to this view.

- 70 percent of the elite respondents have stated that MGNREGS works are displayed in notice board and 30 percent of the respondents did not subscribe to this view.
- 78 percent of the elite respondents have stated that up to 26 percent of women workers are involved in MGNREGS works and 22 percent of the respondents have stated that 26-50 percent of the women workers are involved in MGNREGS works.
- 34 percent of the elite respondents have stated that MGNREGS is properly integrated with DWACRA and 66 percent of the respondents did not subscribe to this view.
- 68 percent of the elite respondents have stated that through MGNREGS, water conservation and harvesting works worth of up to 50000 rupees is created, and the same is Rs 50000-100000 worth of water conservation and harvesting worth works are created by MGNREGS works as stated by 22 percent and 10 percent of the respondents have stated that the same is above 100000 rupees.
- 58 percent of the sample elite respondents have stated that up to 25000 rupees worth flood control and protection assets are created through MGNREGS works and the same is worth of 25000-50000 rupees as endorsed by 28 percent of the respondents and above 50000 rupees as endorsed by 14 percent respondents.
- 24 percent of the sample elite respondents have stated that up to one lakh rupees worth micro irrigation assets are created through MGNREGS works and the same is worth of above one lakh rupees as endorsed by 76 percent of the respondents.
- 16 percent of the sample elite respondents have stated that up to 20000 rupees worth of land development works of SCs and STs are completed through MGNREGS, 24 percent of the elite respondents have stated that 20000-40000 rupees worth of land

development works of SCs and STs have been completed and the same is worth above 40000 rupees is created through MGNREGS.

- Through MGNREGS, rural connectivity worth of up to 50000 rupees worth works are created which is endorsed by 68 percent of the elite respondents followed by 50000-100000 rupees worth work s created by 20 percent of the respondents and above 100000 worth rural connectivity is created by 12 percent of the respondents.
- Through MGNREGS, other works worth of up to 10000 rupees worth works are created which is endorsed by 64 percent of the elite respondents followed by 10000-20000 rupees worth work s created by 22 percent of the respondents and above 20000 worth other works is created by 14 percent of the respondents.
- Transparency is maintained in muster roll management which is endorsed by 74 percent of the elite respondents and 26 percent of the respondents did not subscribe to this view.
- 96 percent of the elite respondents have stated that MGNREGS works are selected by Gram Sabha and 4 percent of the elite respondents have stated that the MGNREGS works are selected by officials.
- 66 percent of the elite respondents have stated that community assets are improved due to MGNREGS and the same is constant in the case of 22 percent of the elite respondents and declined as endorsed by 12 percent of the elite respondents.
- **The first hypothesis** "The performance of MGNREGS is socially neutral" is accepted.
- **The second hypothesis** "Governance practices in MGNREGS are poor" is accepted.

SUGGESTIONS

On the basis of findings and conclusions are drawn, the following suggestions are made to strengthen the program of MGNREGS and to enable the beneficiaries to augment their welfare through the means of the said program which include

1. The number of man-days of employment through MGNREGS must be increased to 200 days.
2. The number of man-days of employment through MGNREGS should be more in drought-prone areas in relation to that command areas.
3. The absolutely poor should get more man-days of employment than those of the poor through MGNREGS.
4. Quality of assets must be improved for the works covered under MGNREGS.
5. The works through MGNREGS must ensure inclusive growth of rural development, especially of marginalized sections by taking up more lands of them to take up MGNREGS works.
6. Female-headed families must be given number of man-days of employment through MGNREGS.
7. The income of the beneficiaries of MGNREGS must be integrated with micro savings and insurance schemes.
8. The beneficiaries of MGNREGS must take part in Gram Sabha and must take the responsibility of giving useful feedback in Gram Sabha with regard to quality of works in MGNREGS so as to make the institution of Gram Sabha more relevant and efficient.

9. Village-specific research must be encouraged to identify the merits and limitations of this program and in turn to reformulate and rescheduling the works through MGNREGS.
10. MGNREGS must be made an effective instrument of micro-planning with a goal of attaining compatibility between means and ends of rural development.
11. MGNREGS must design programs and works to suit to the requirements of differently abled persons whose services are hitherto neglected.
12. MGNREGS so far has empowered women as workers but not women as the community. Hence, MGNREGS must strive to emulate policies and programs to ensure women empowerment on a community basis.

AREAS OF FURTHER RESEARCH

- MGNREGS and its contribution to women social empowerment
- How to design MGNREGS to suit to the employment requirements of otherwise abled persons
- The role of citizen audit in complementing social audit to strengthen the process of MGNREGS